This book belongs to

. . . .

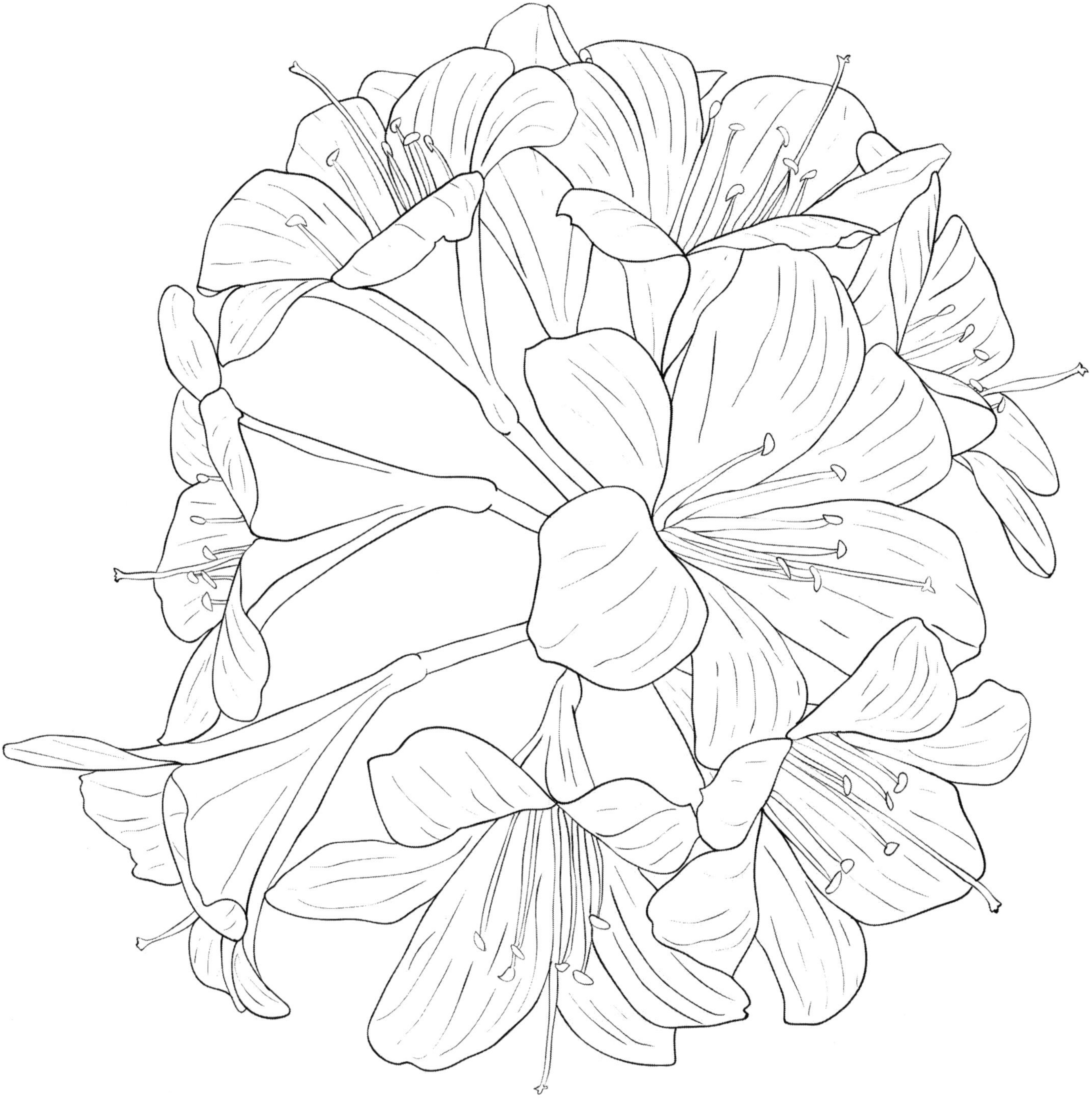

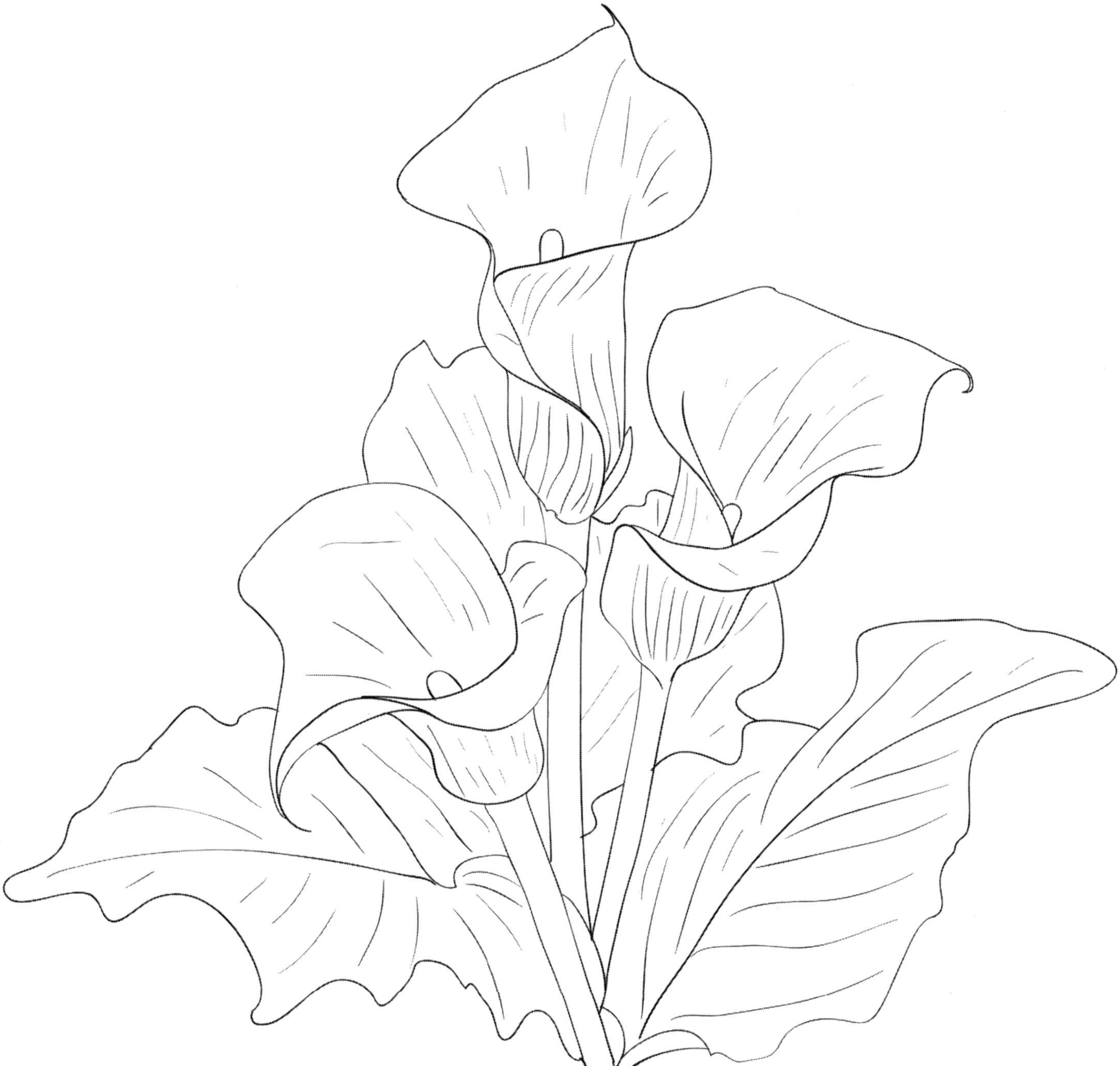

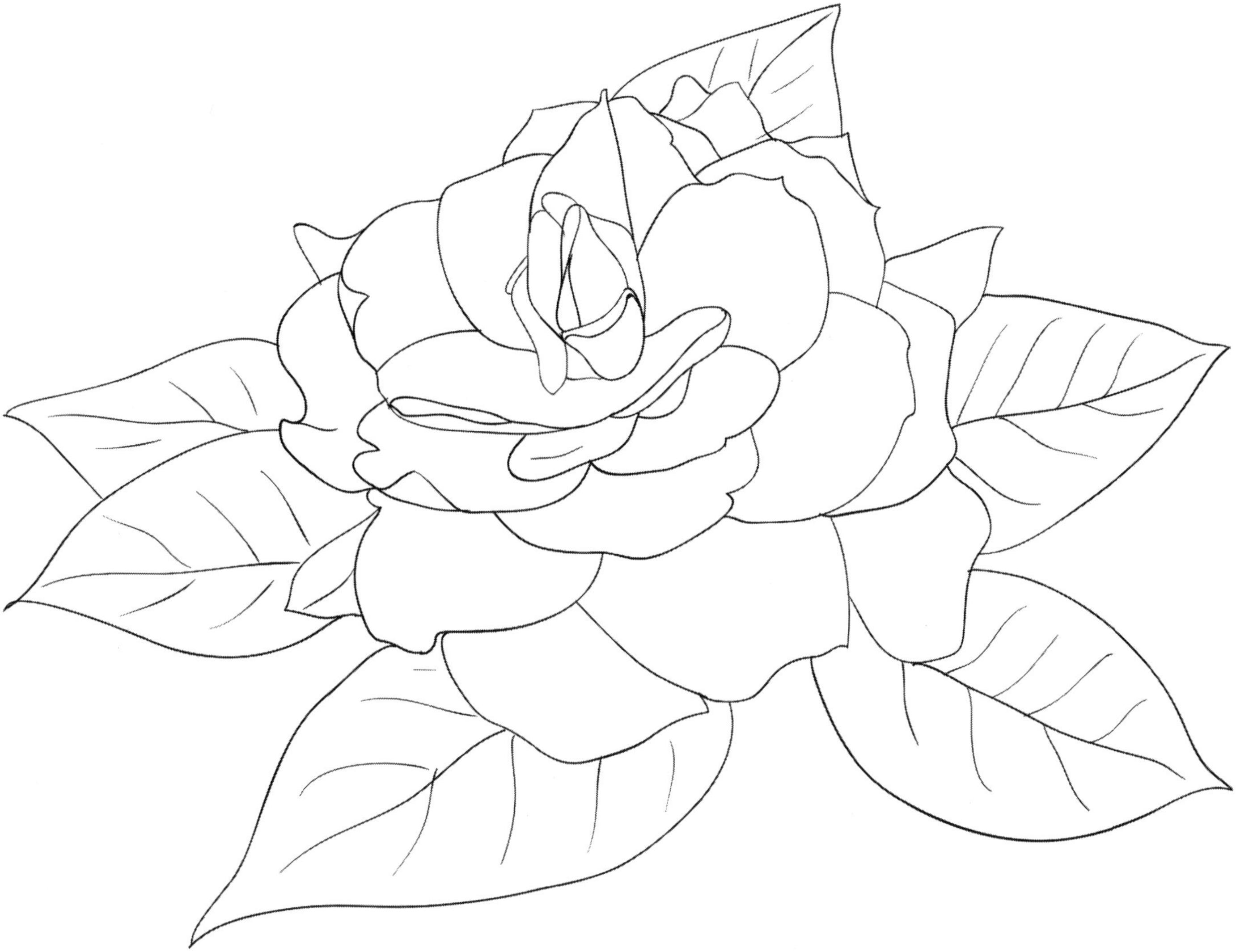

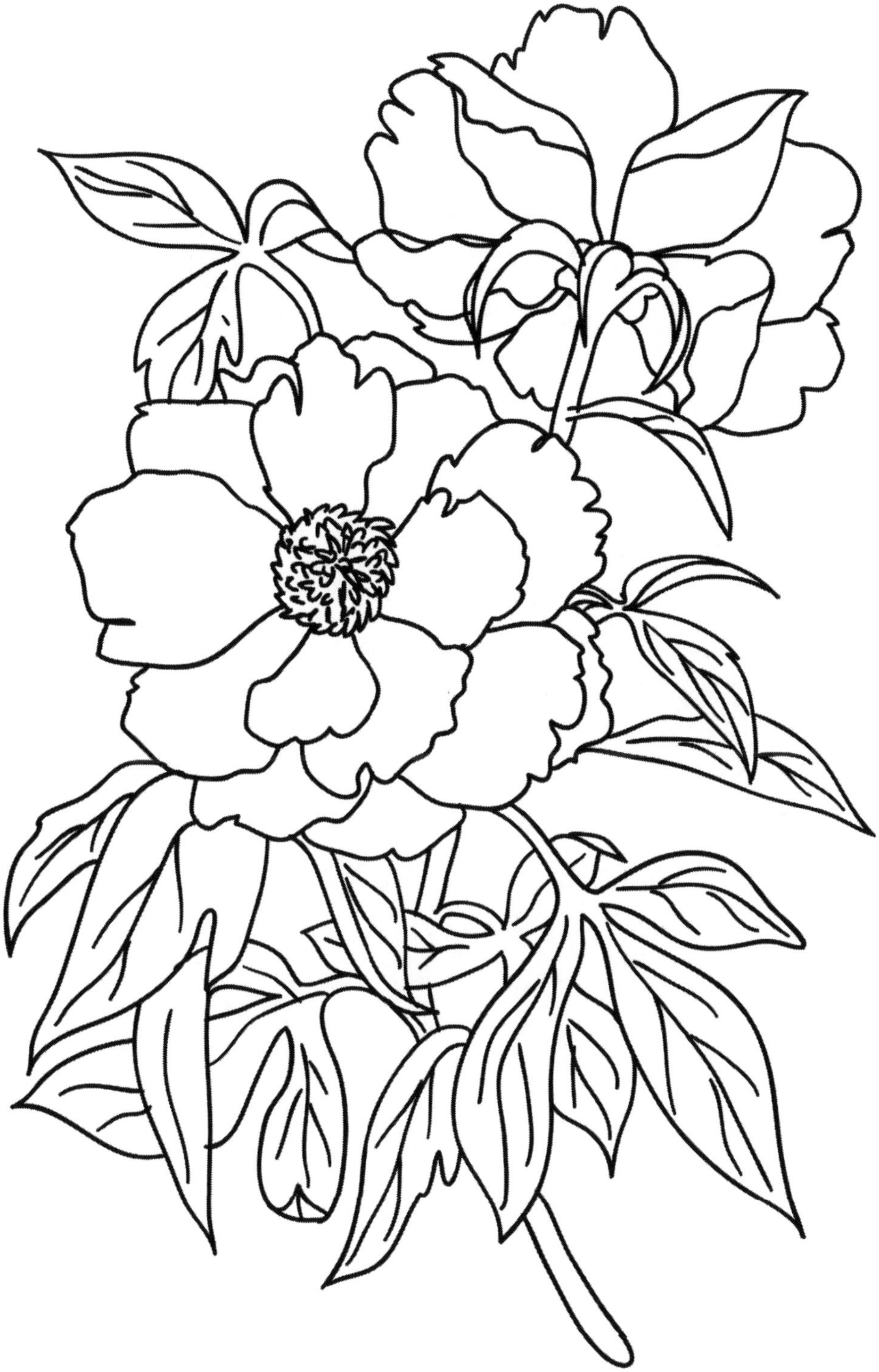

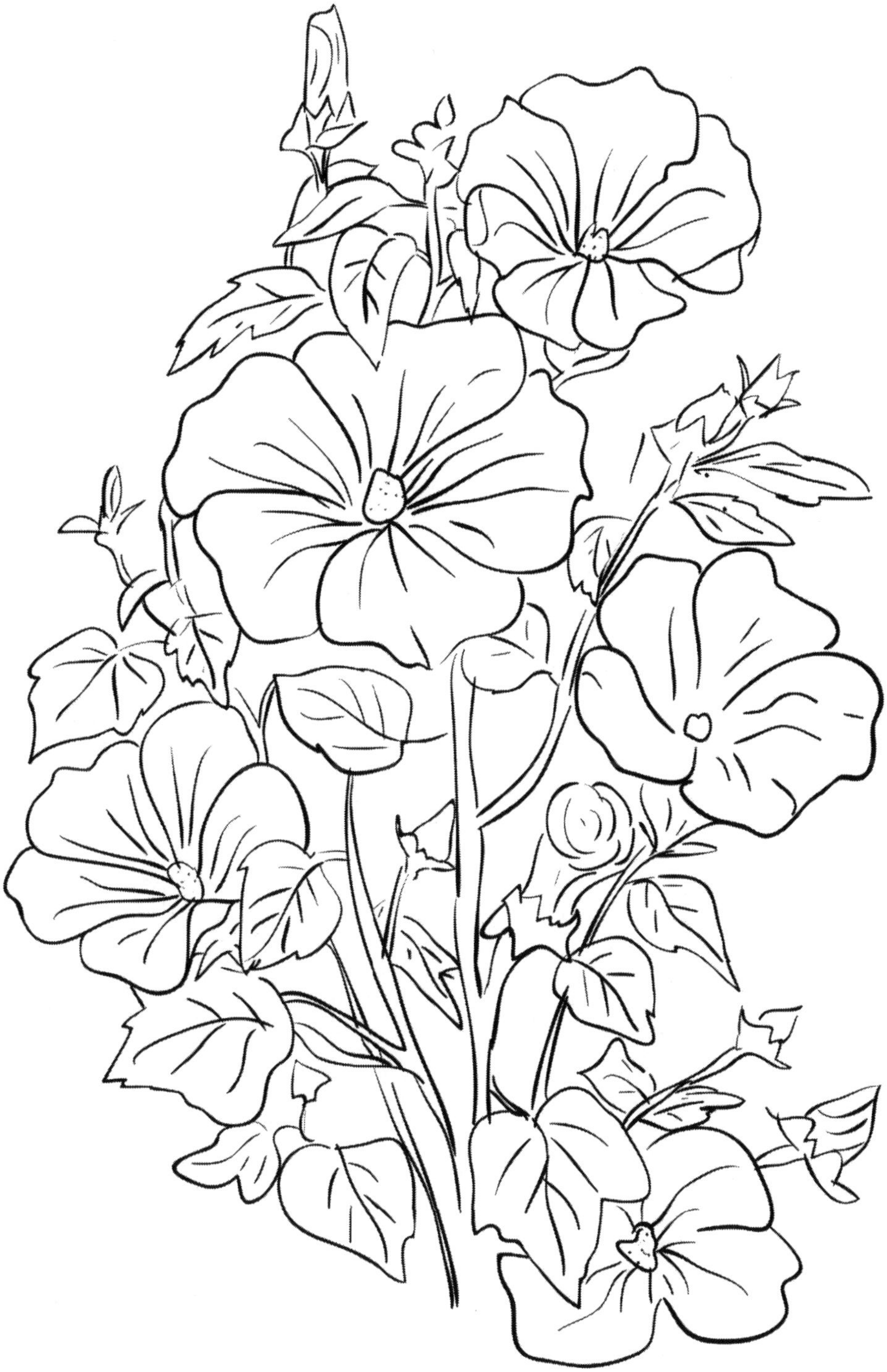

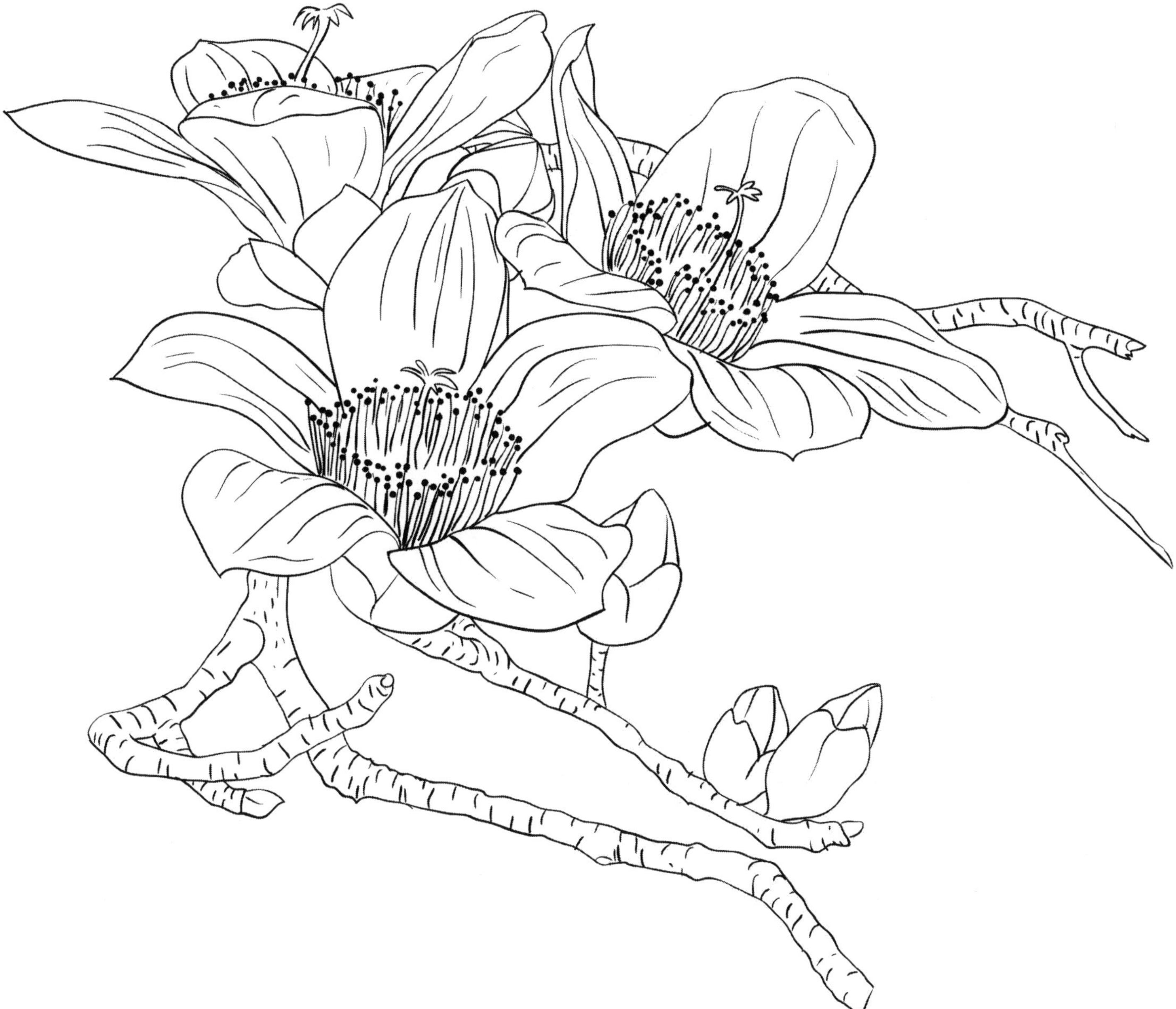

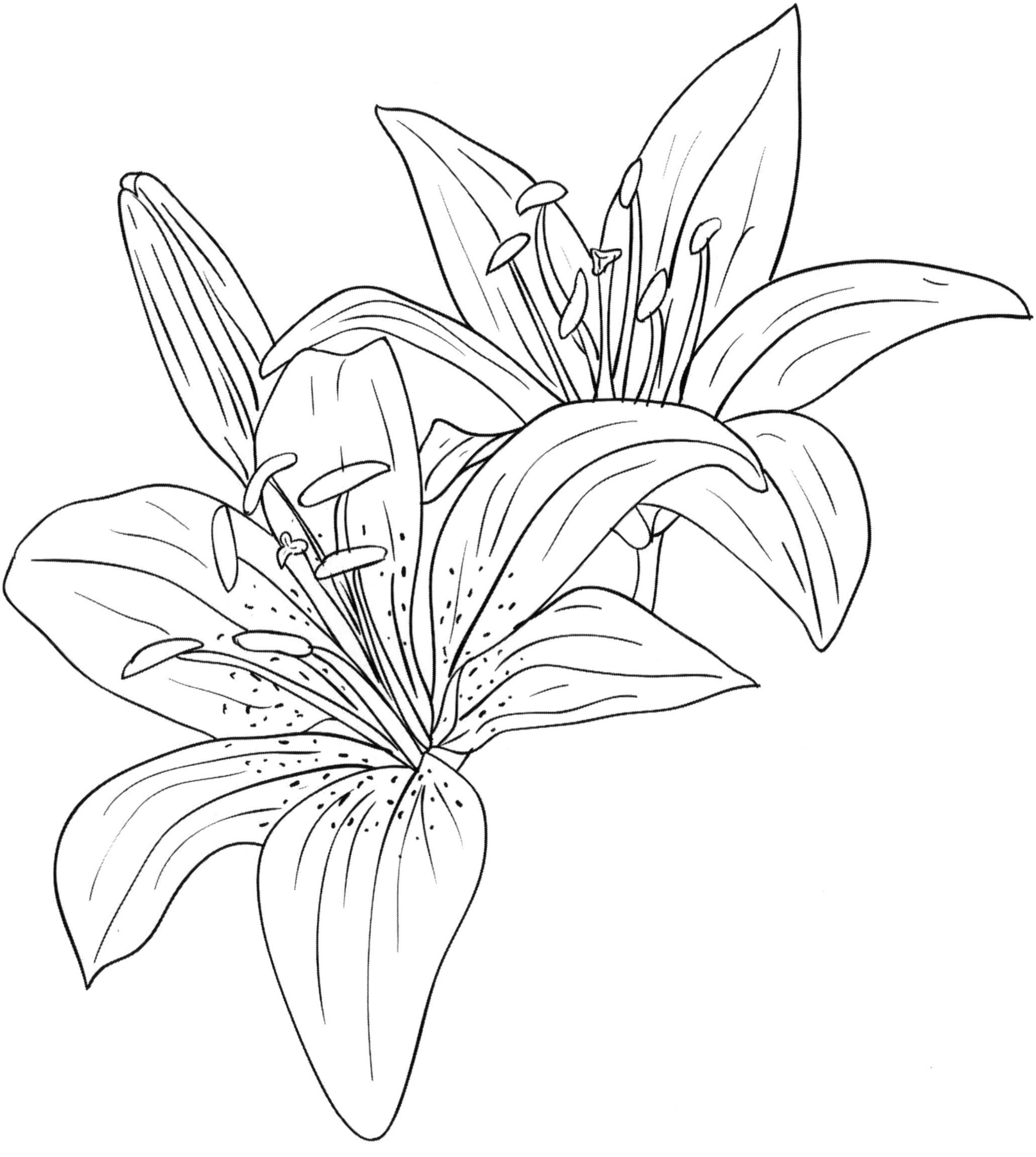

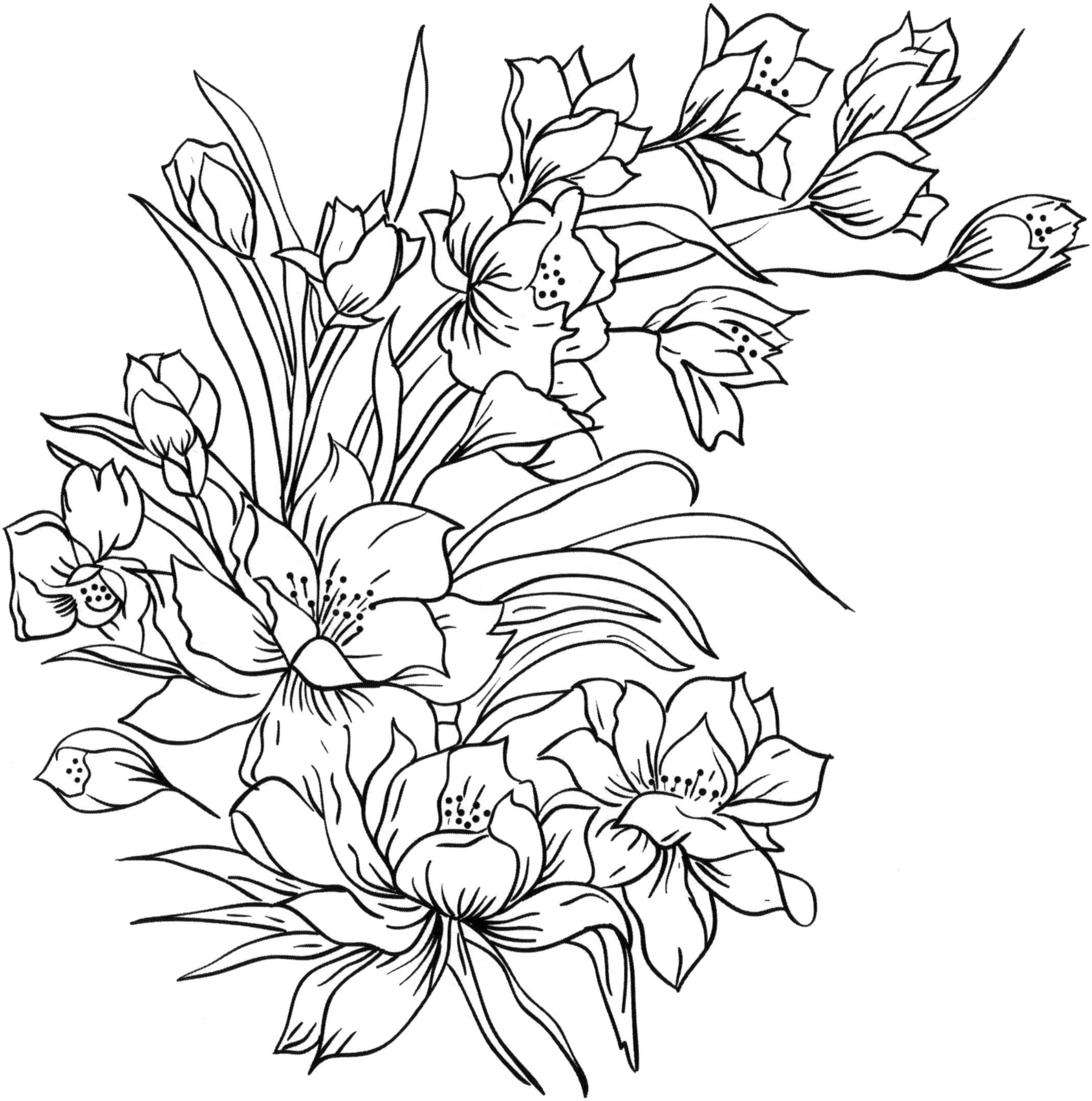

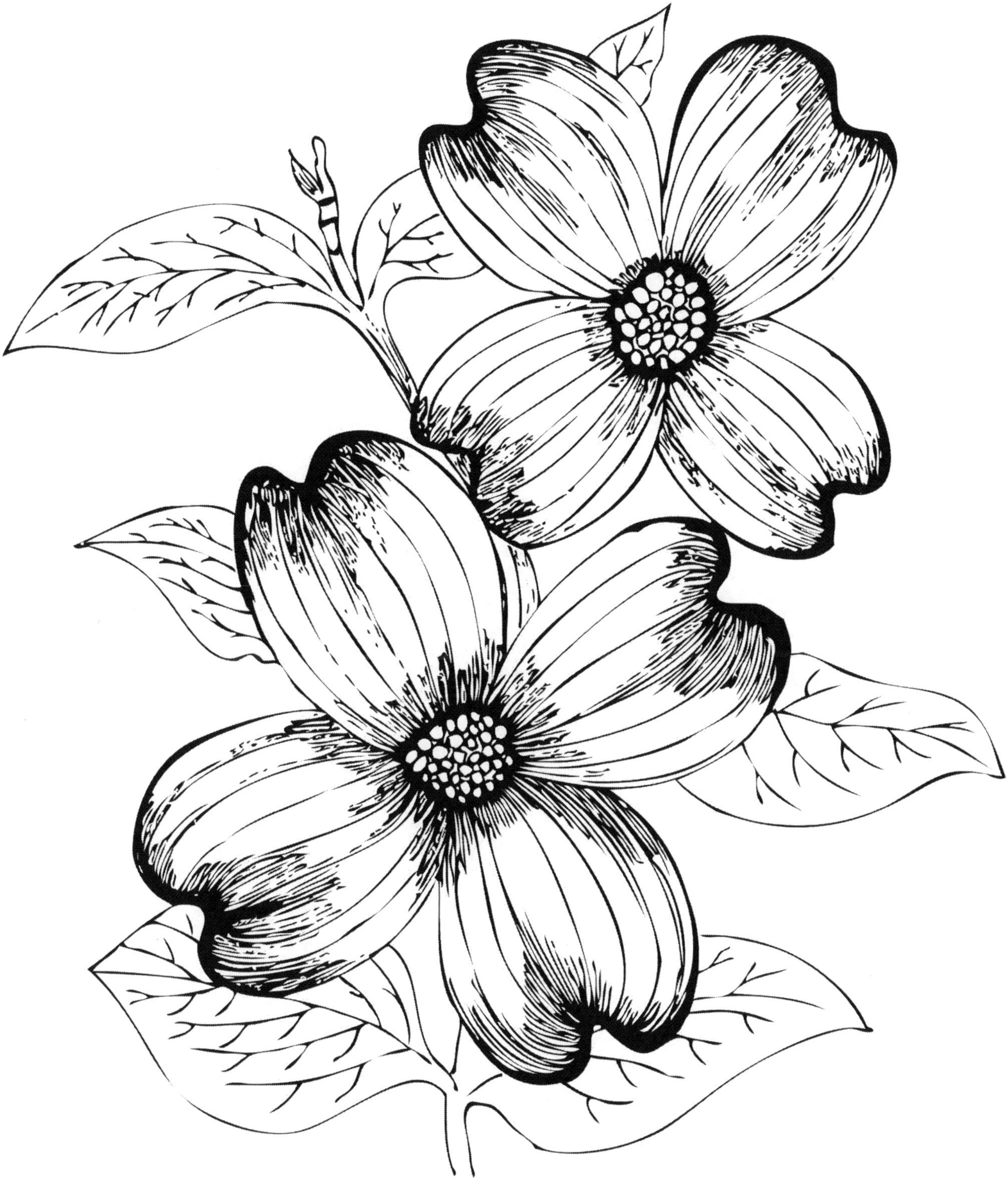

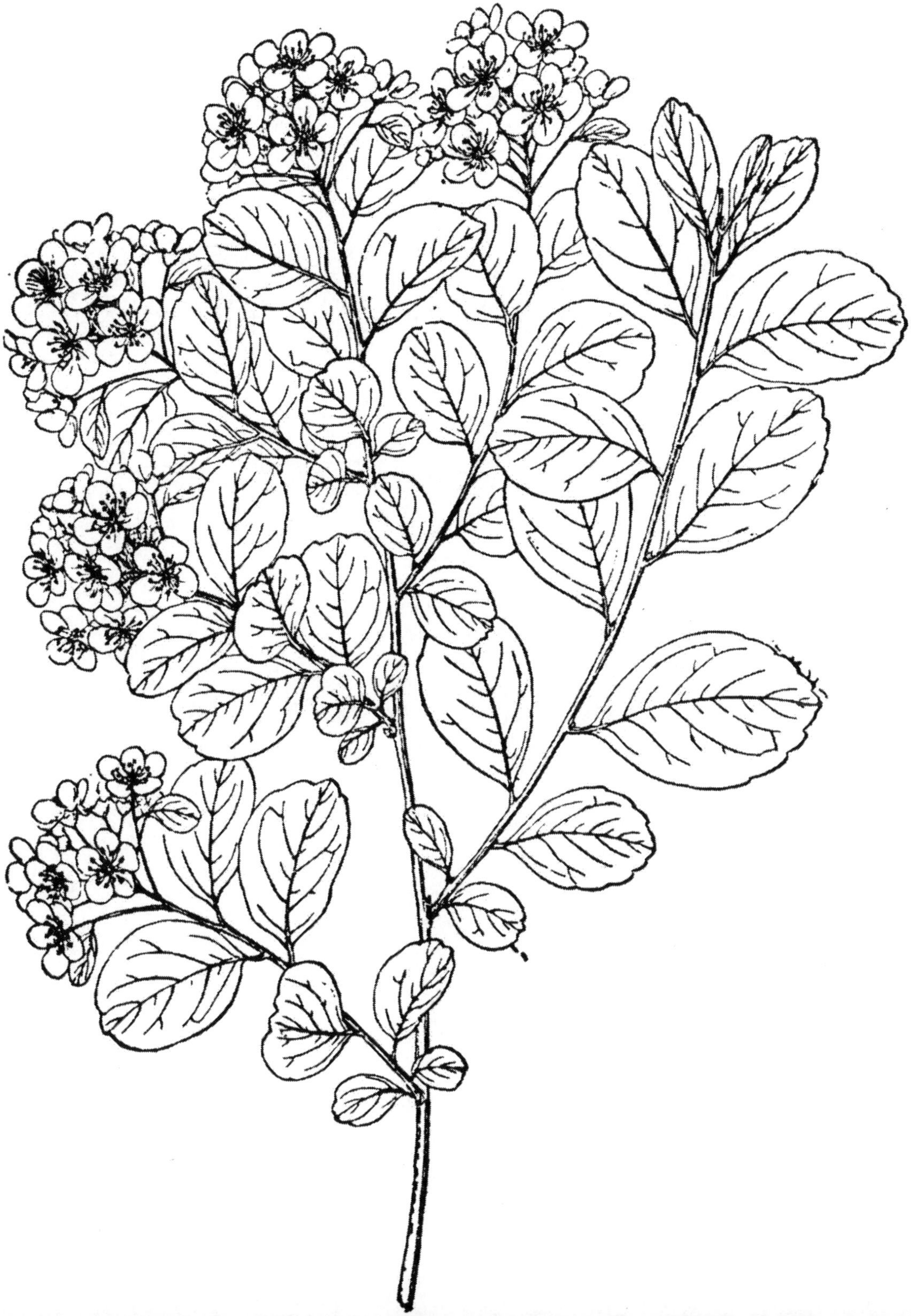

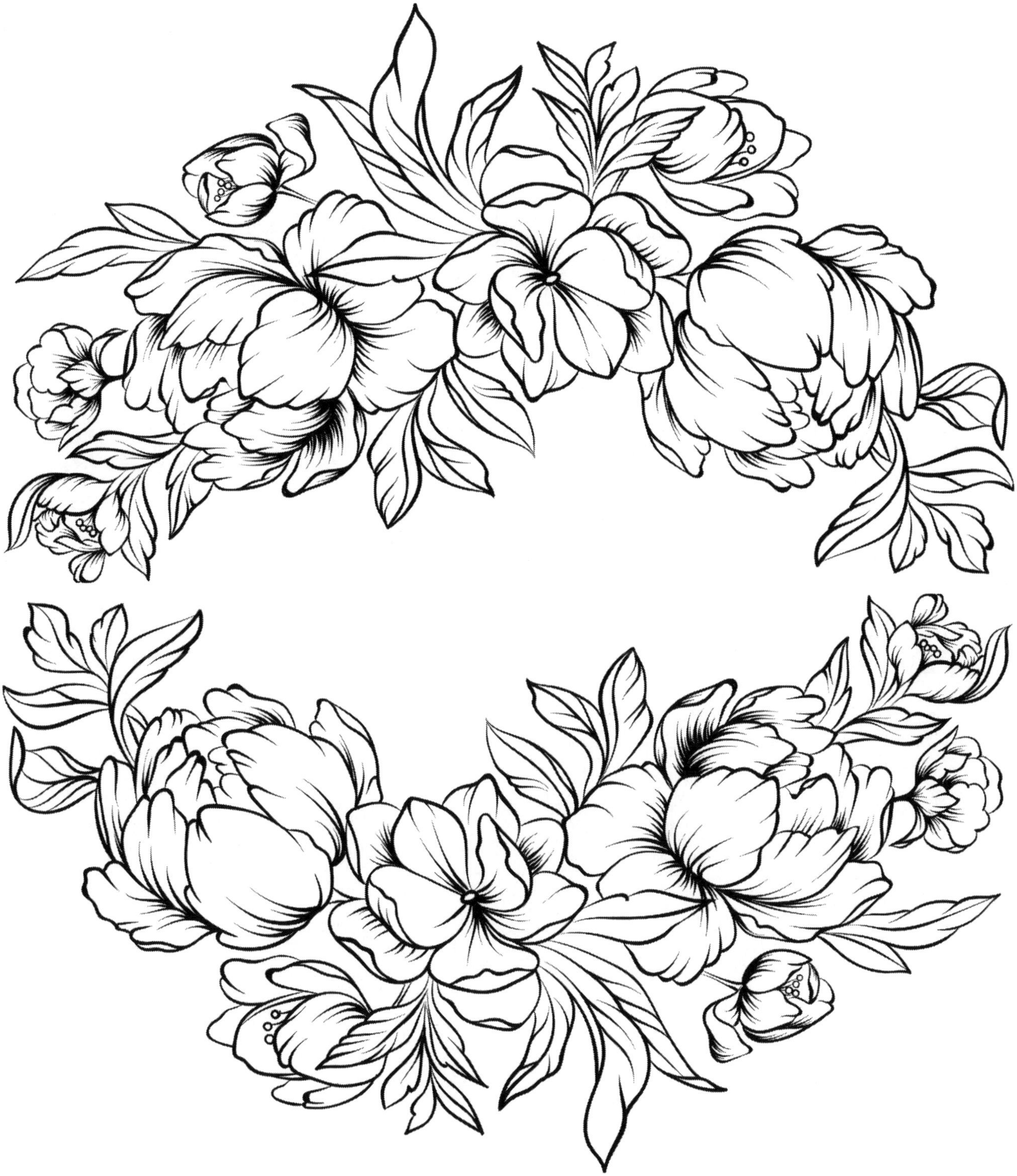

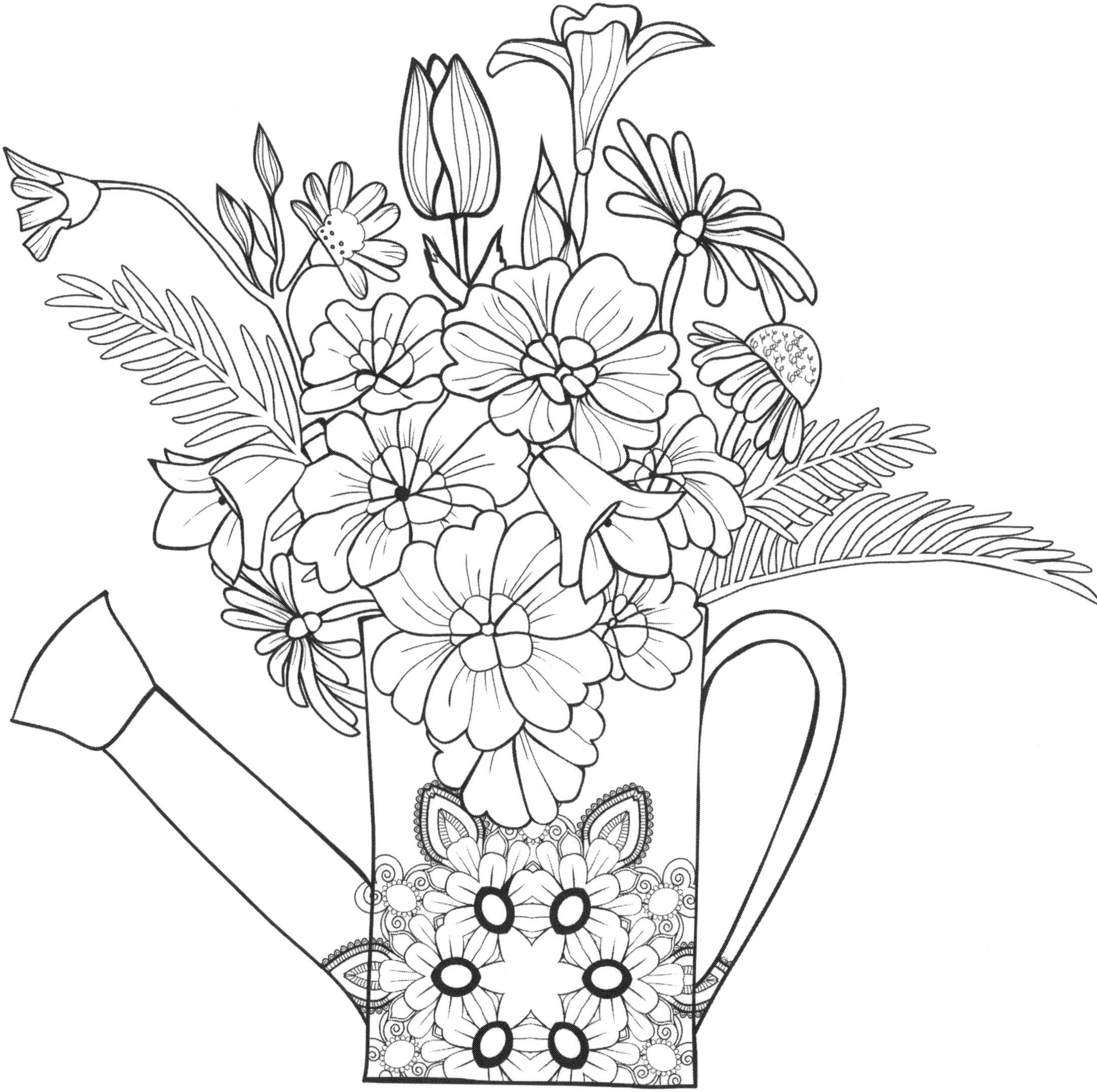

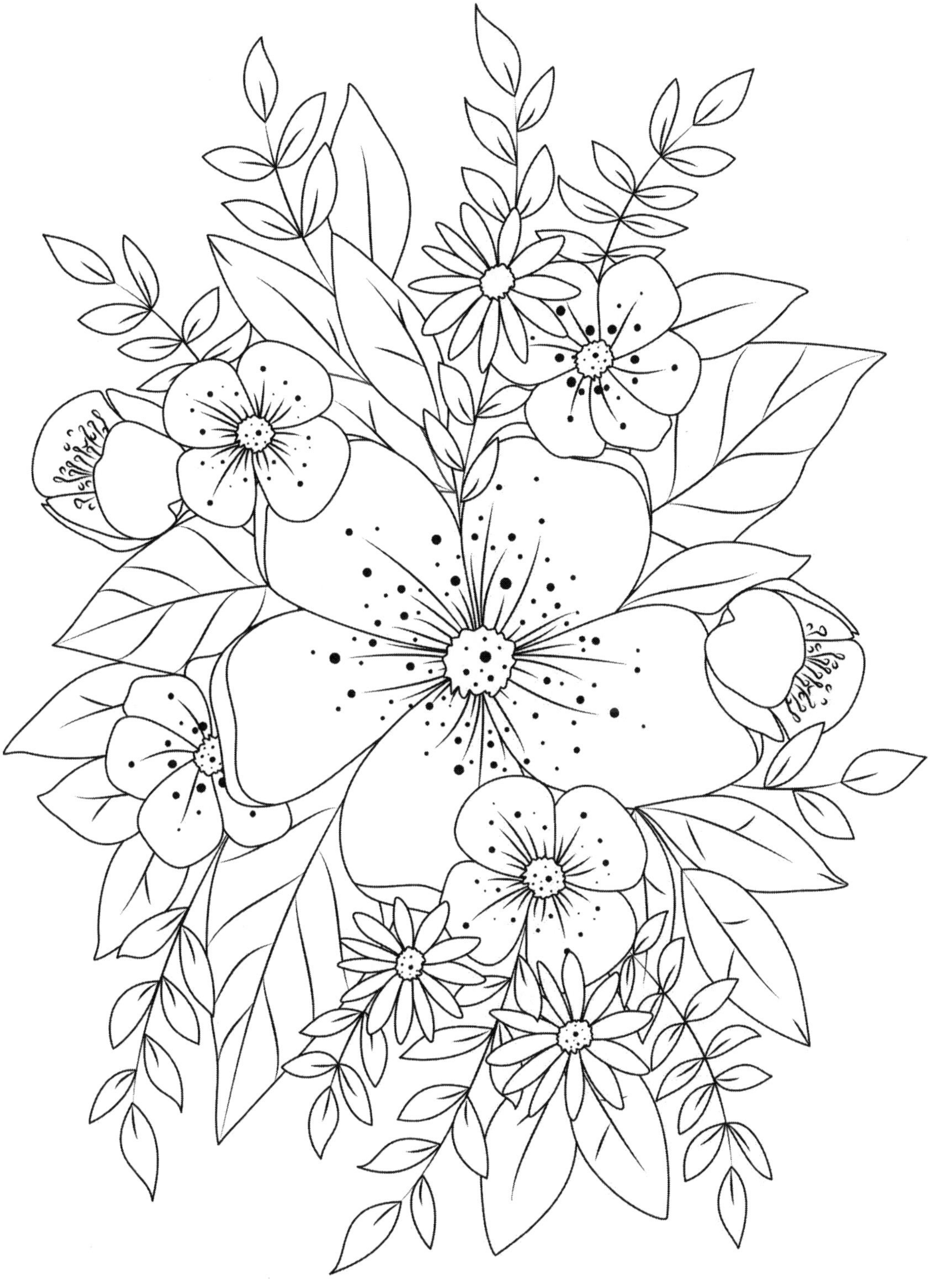

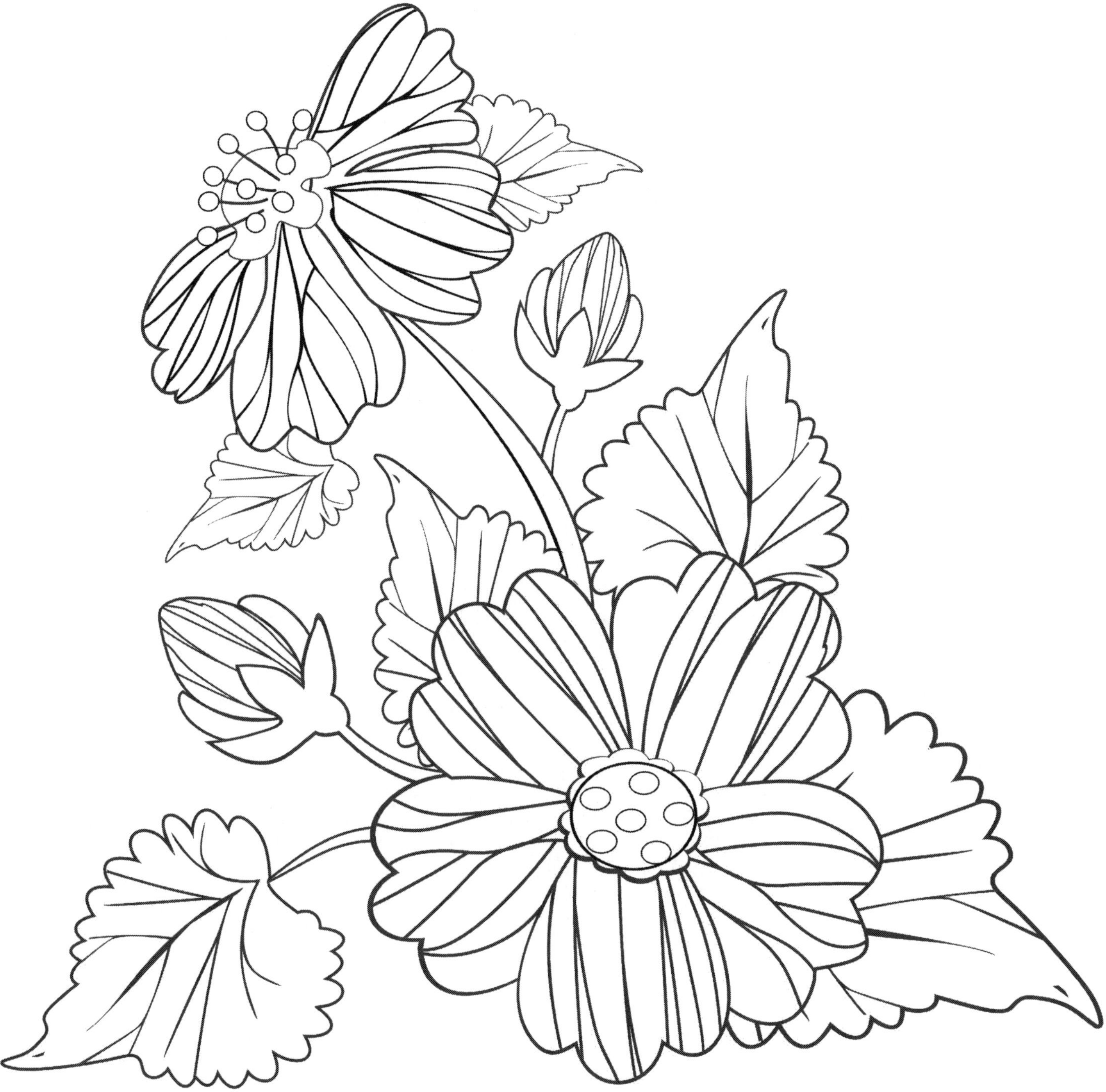

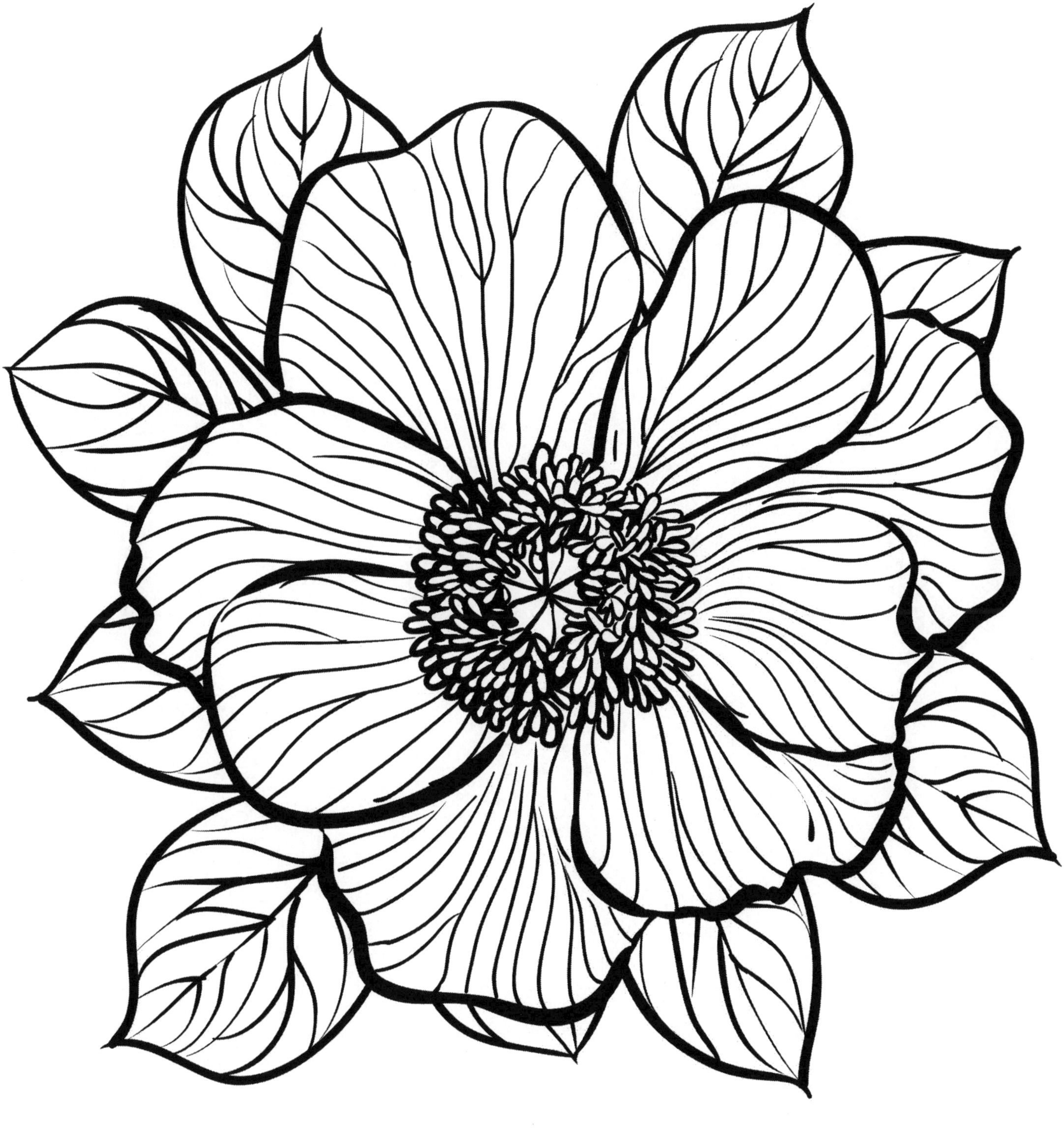

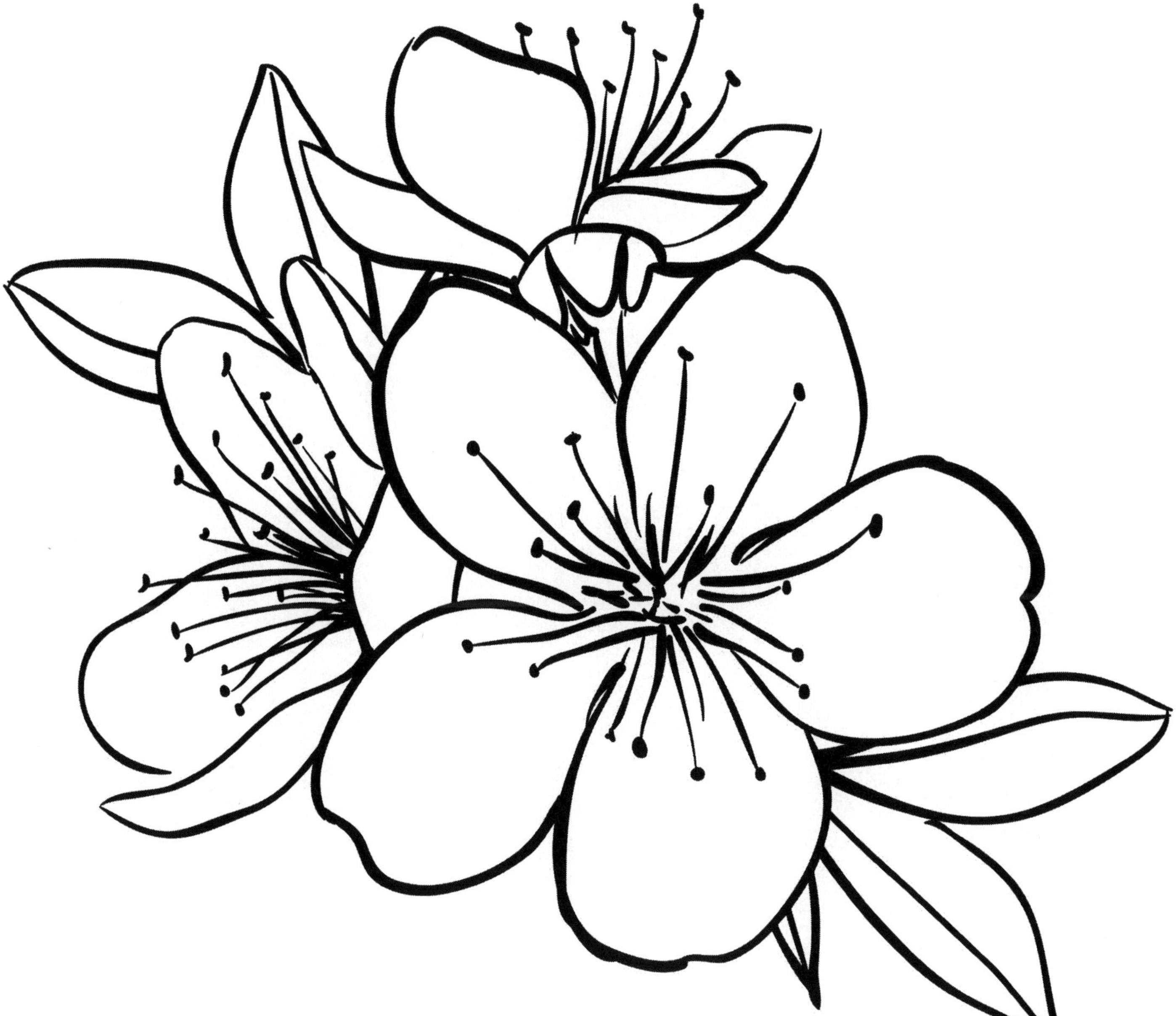

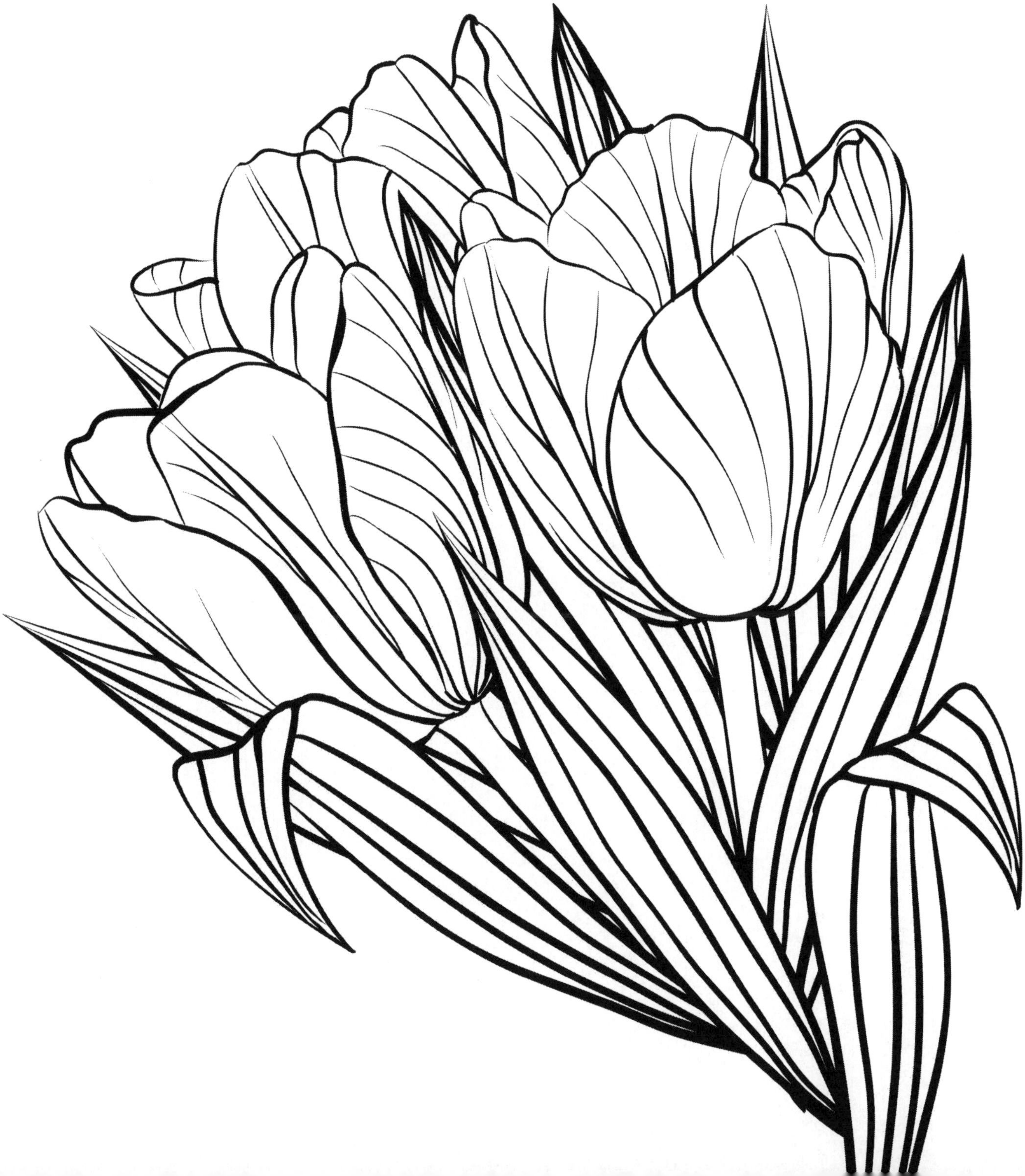

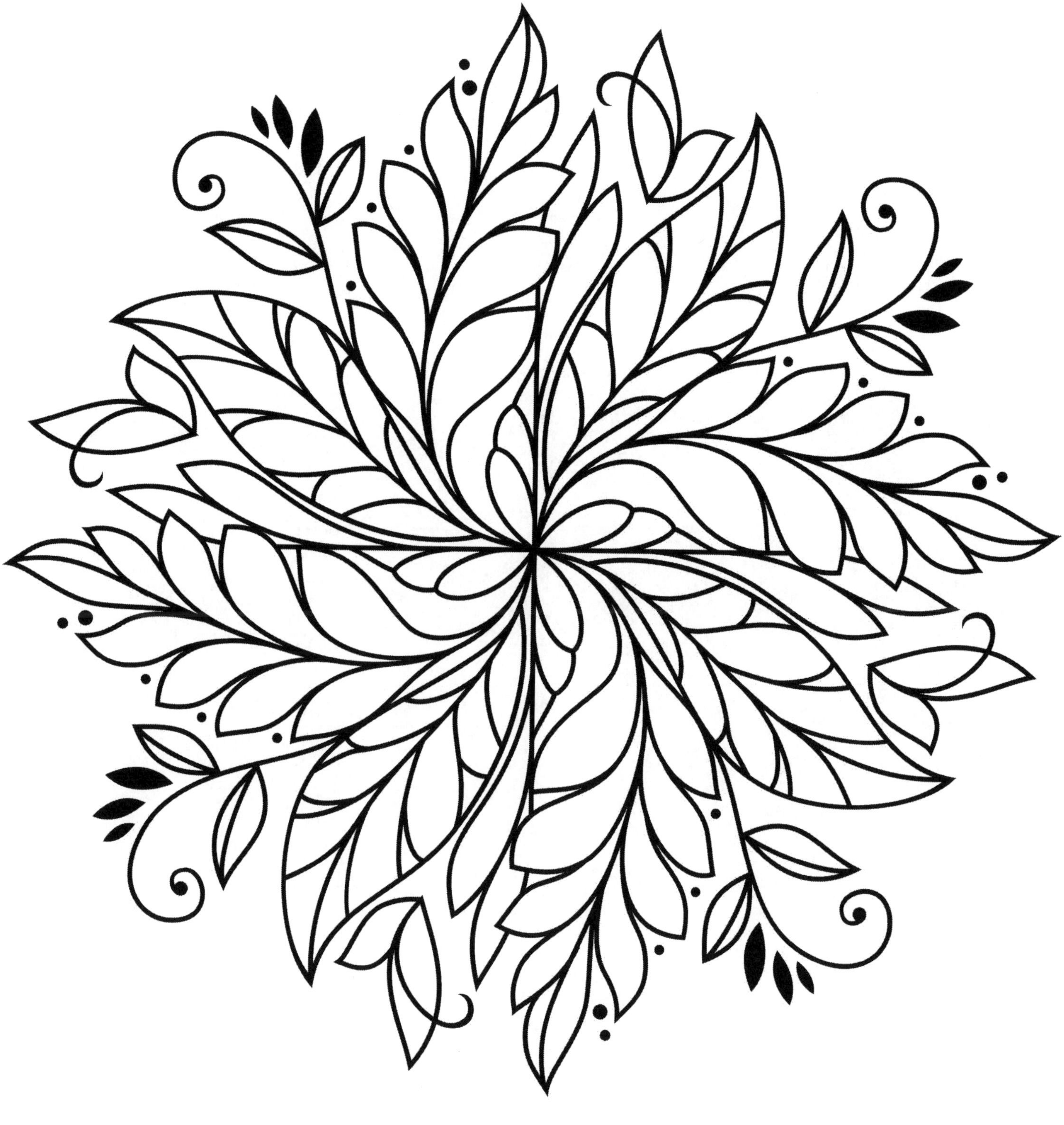

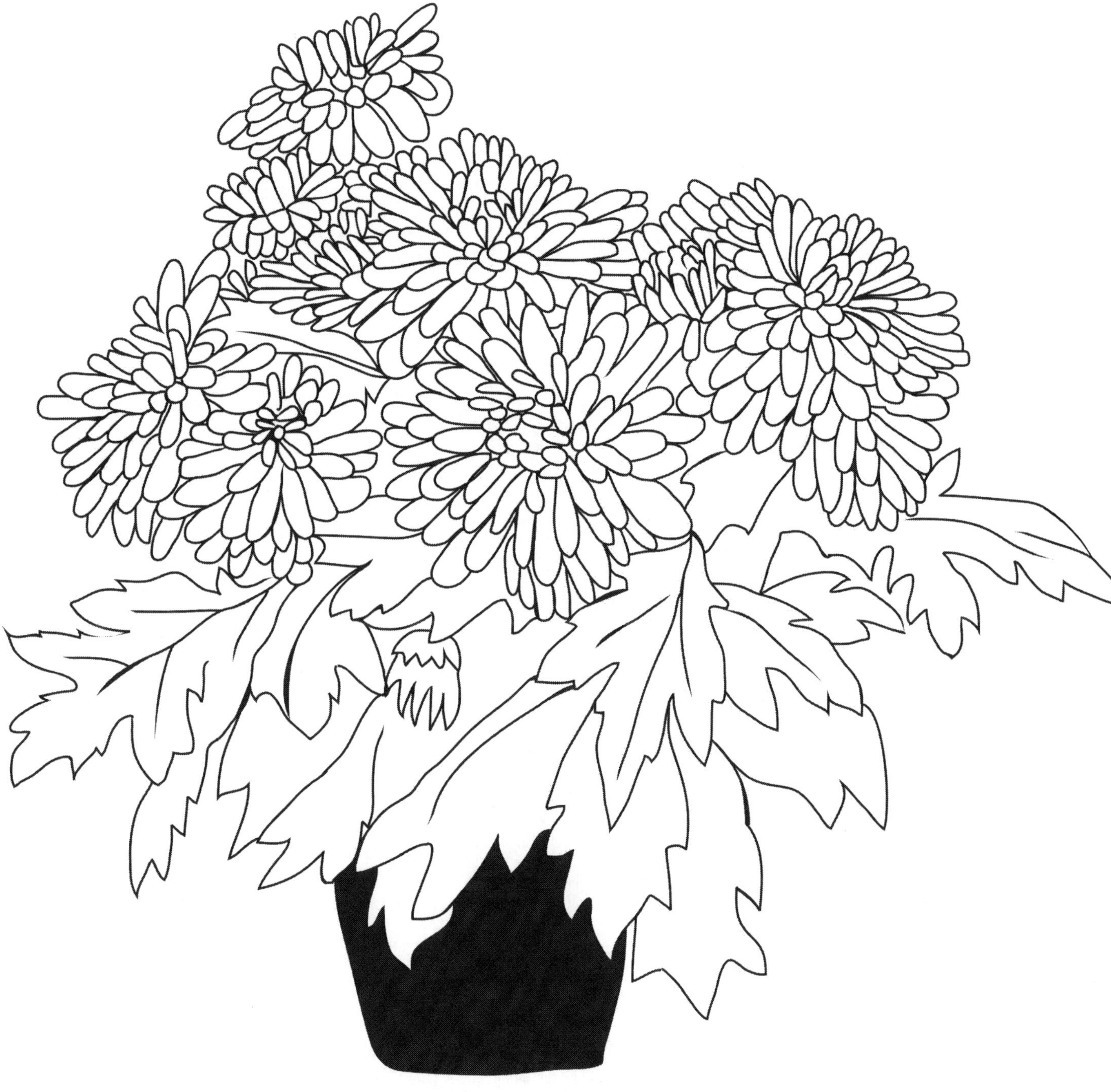

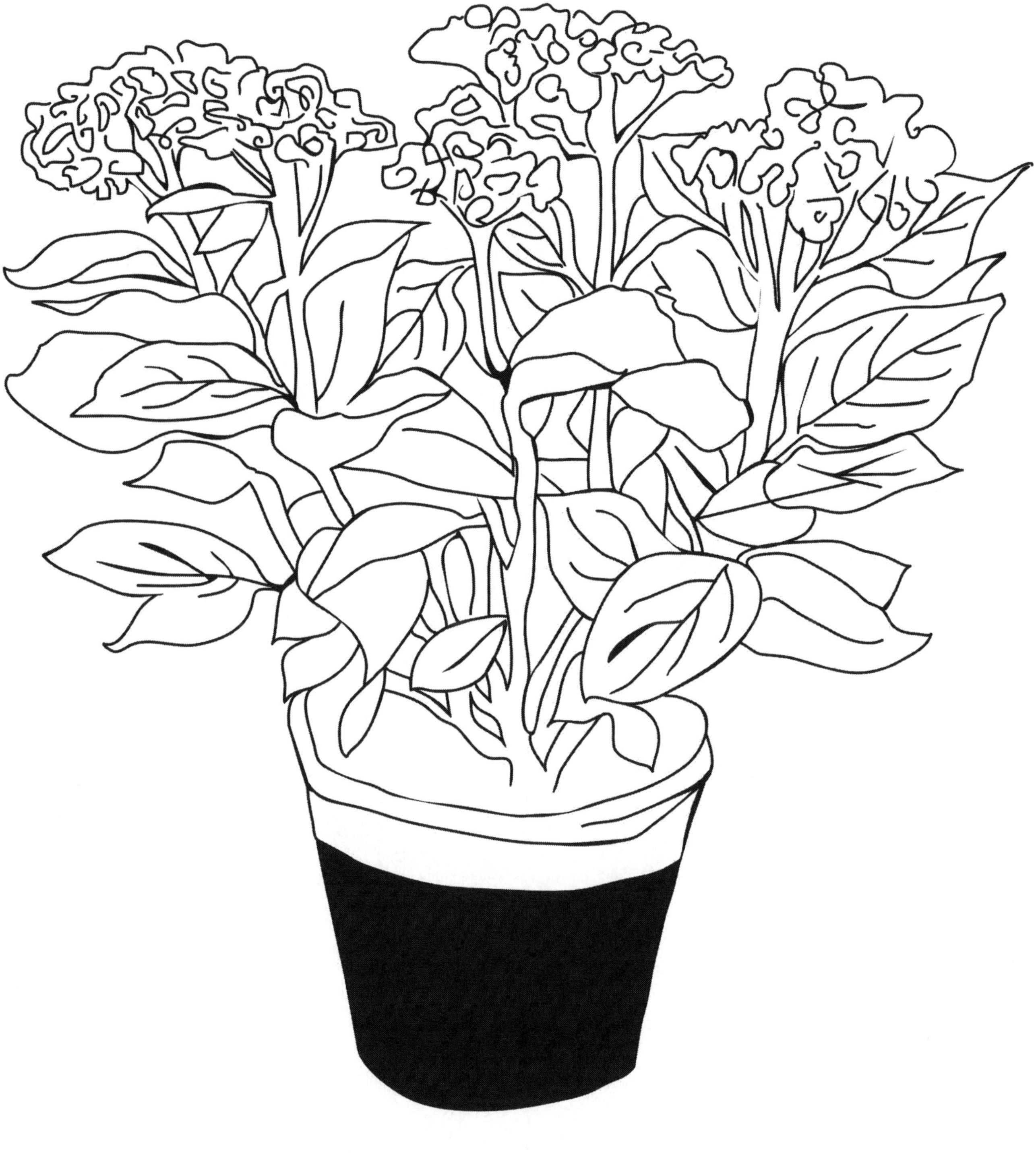

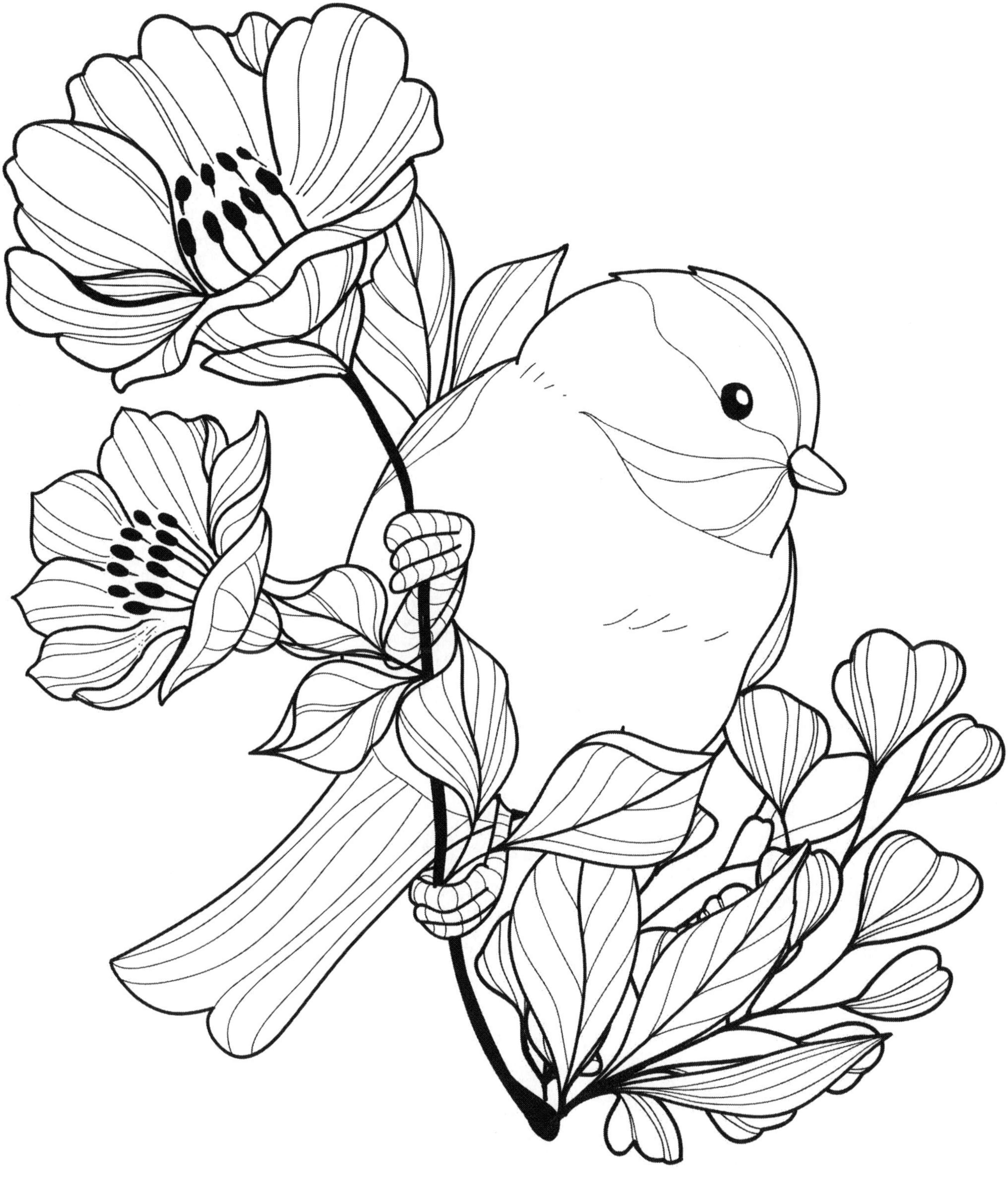

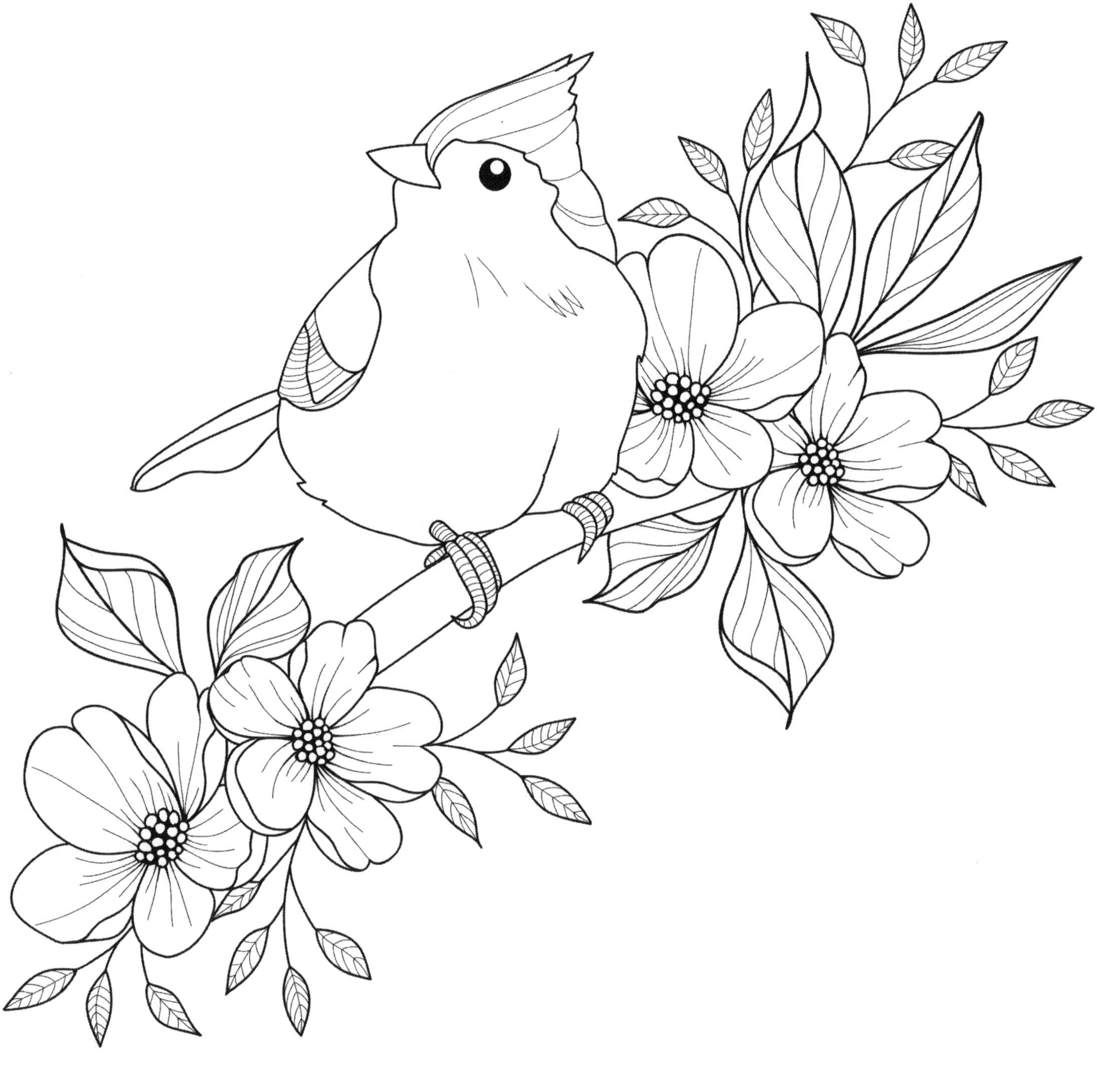

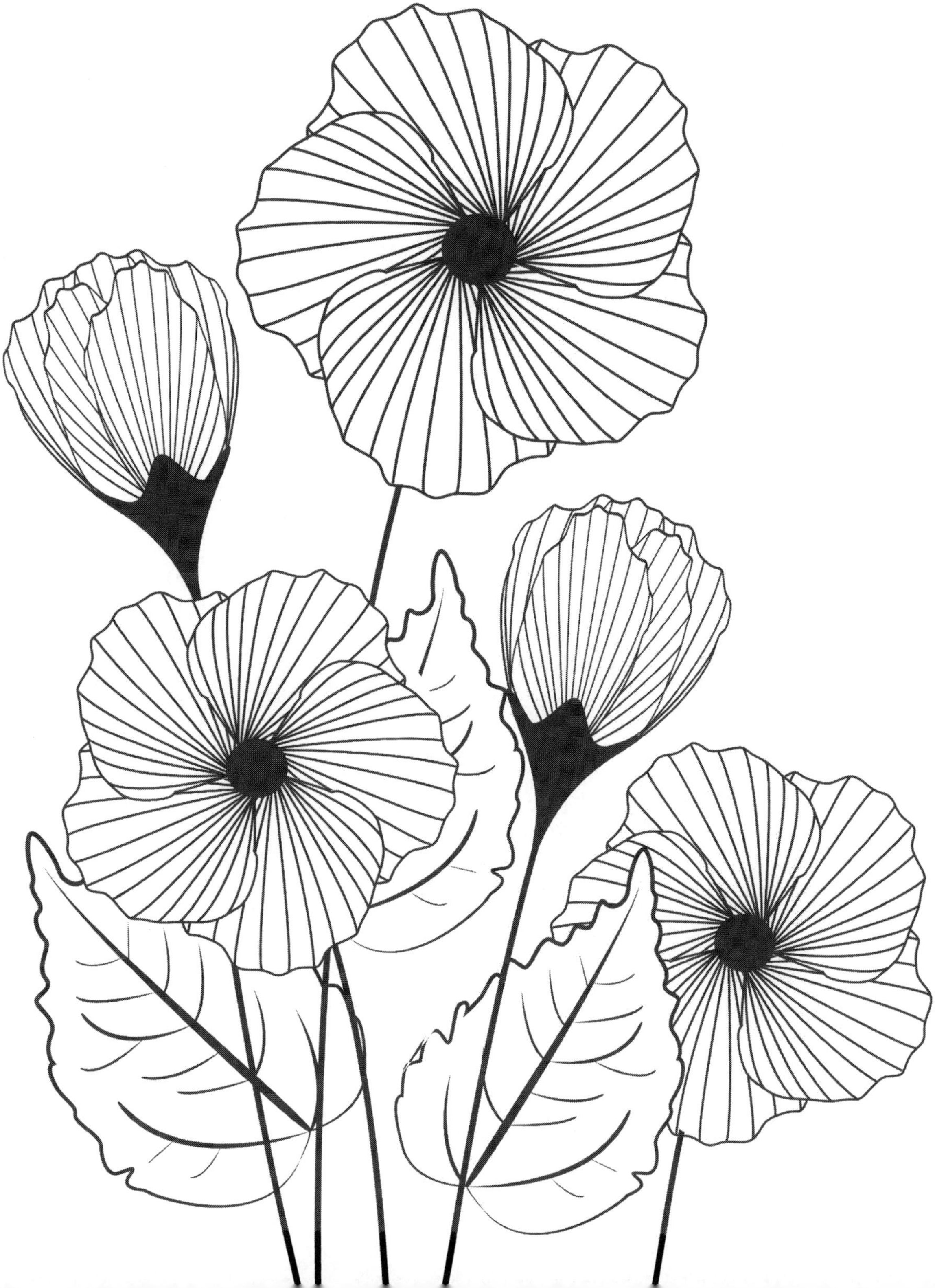

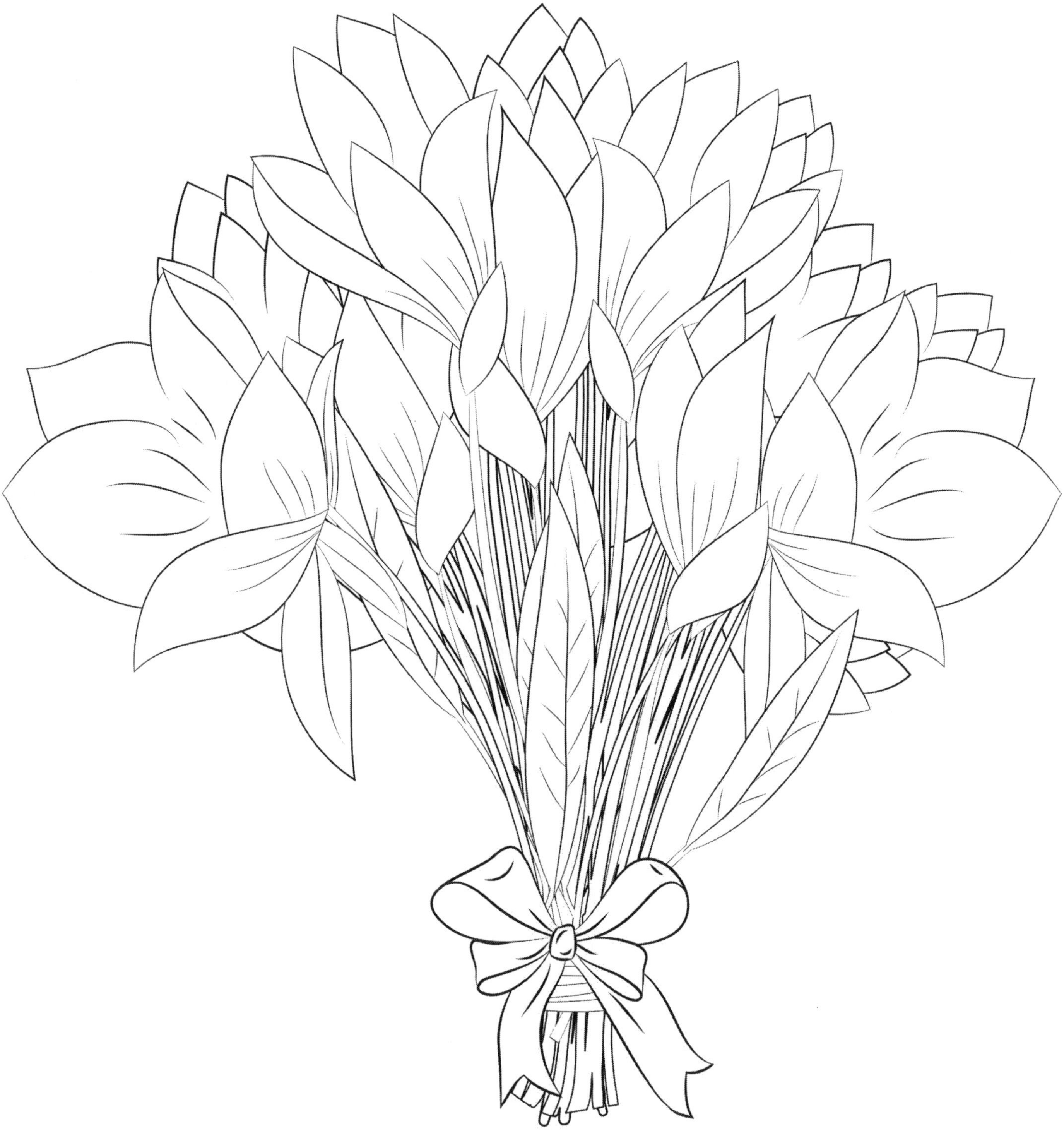

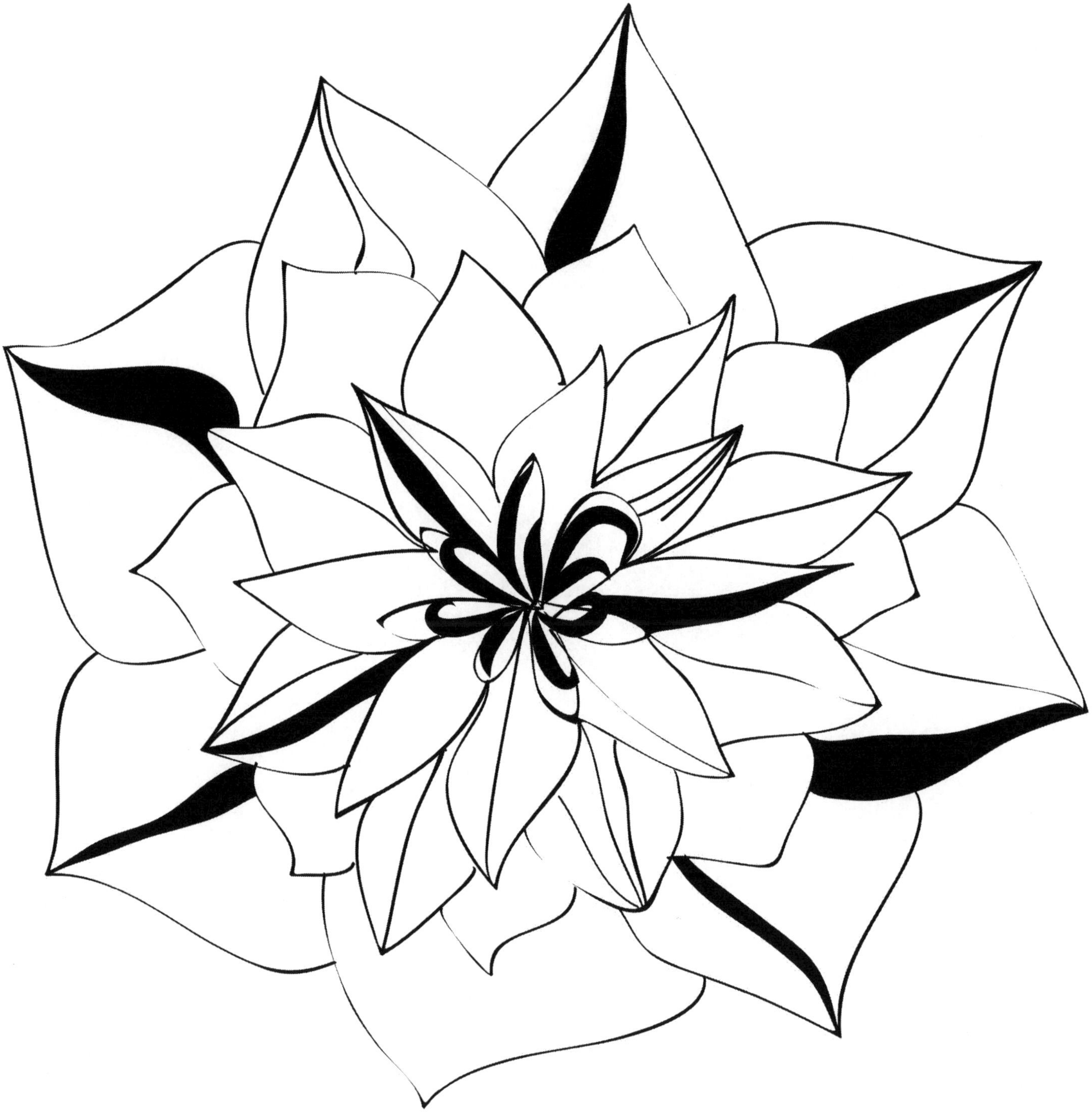

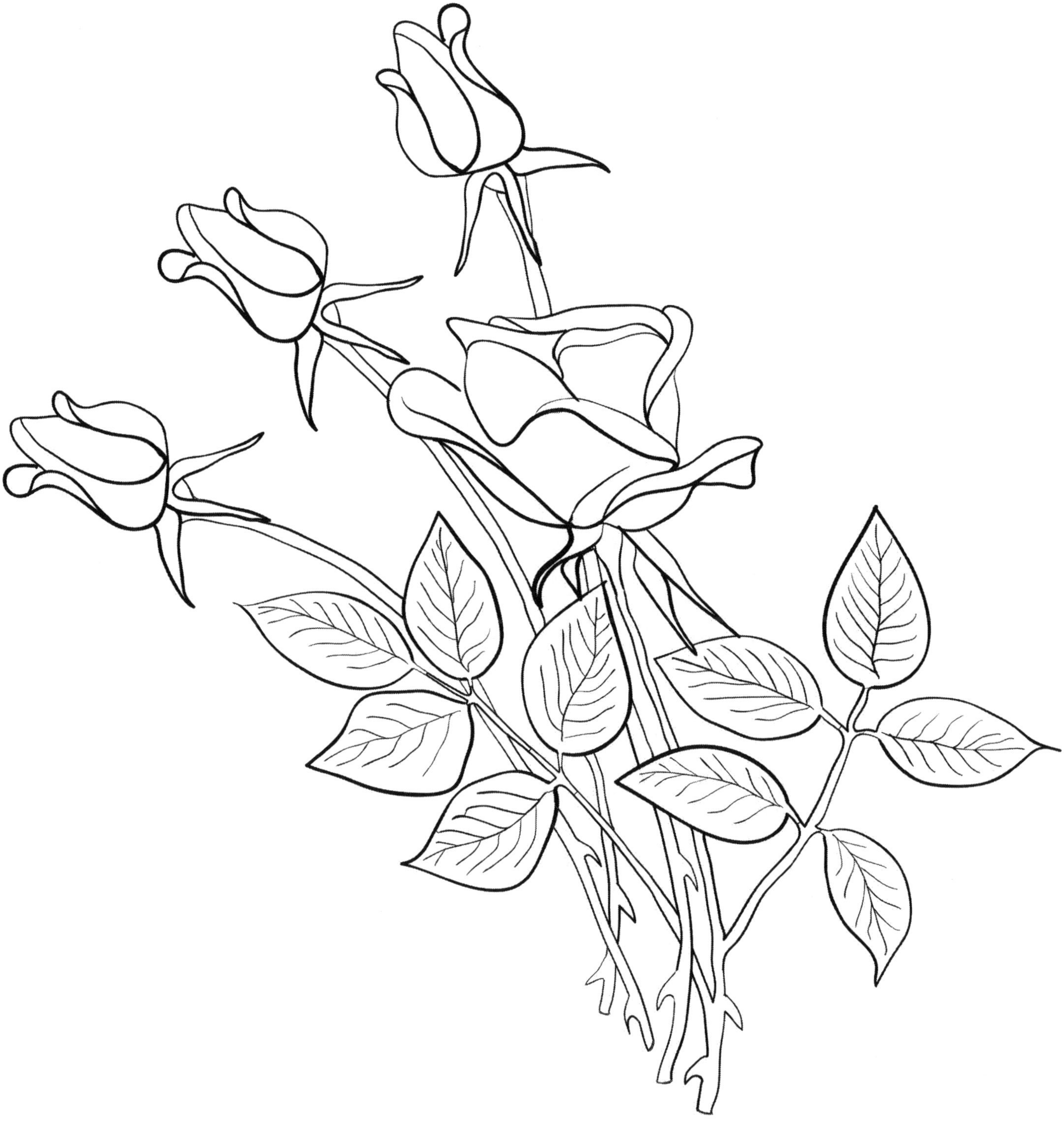

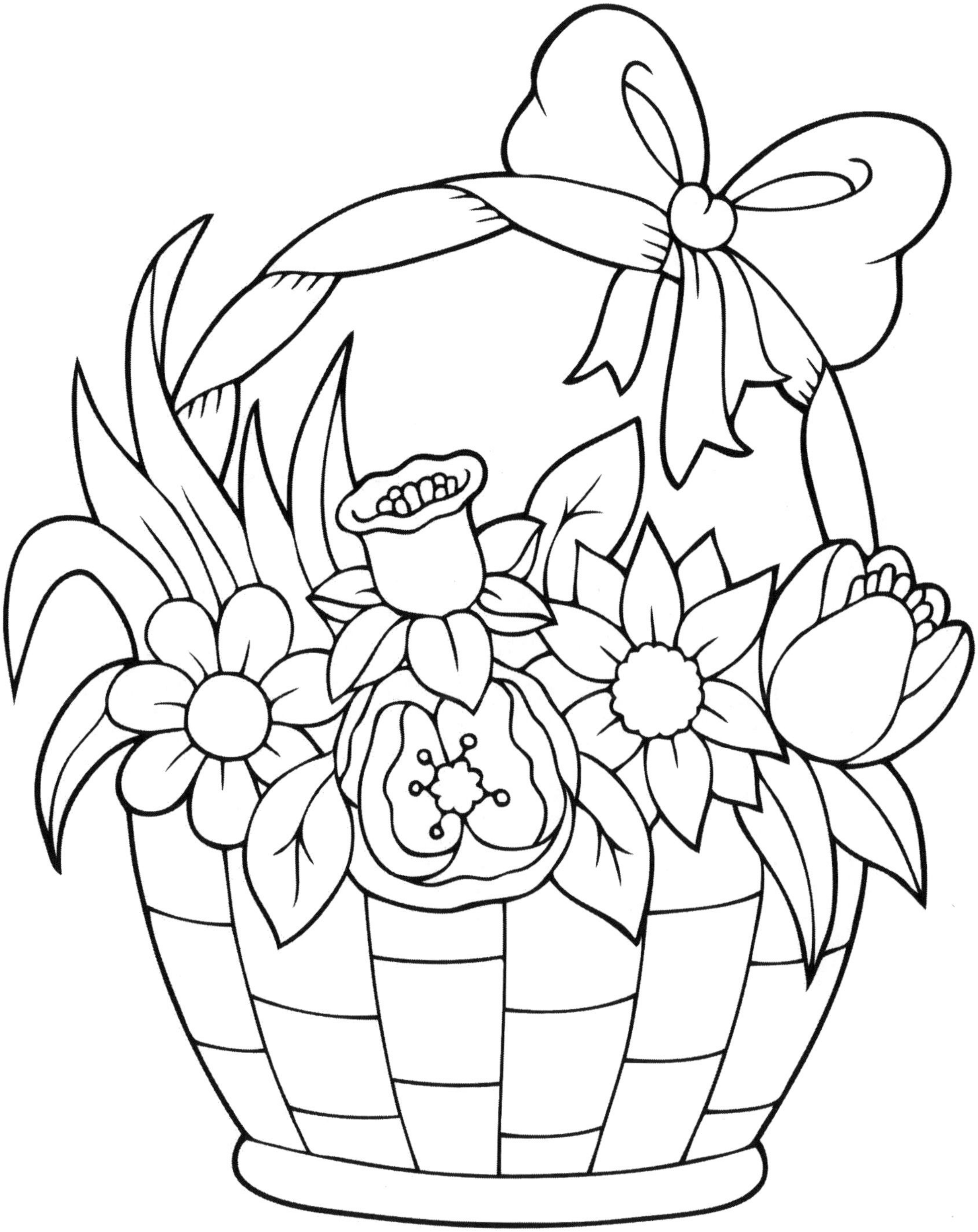

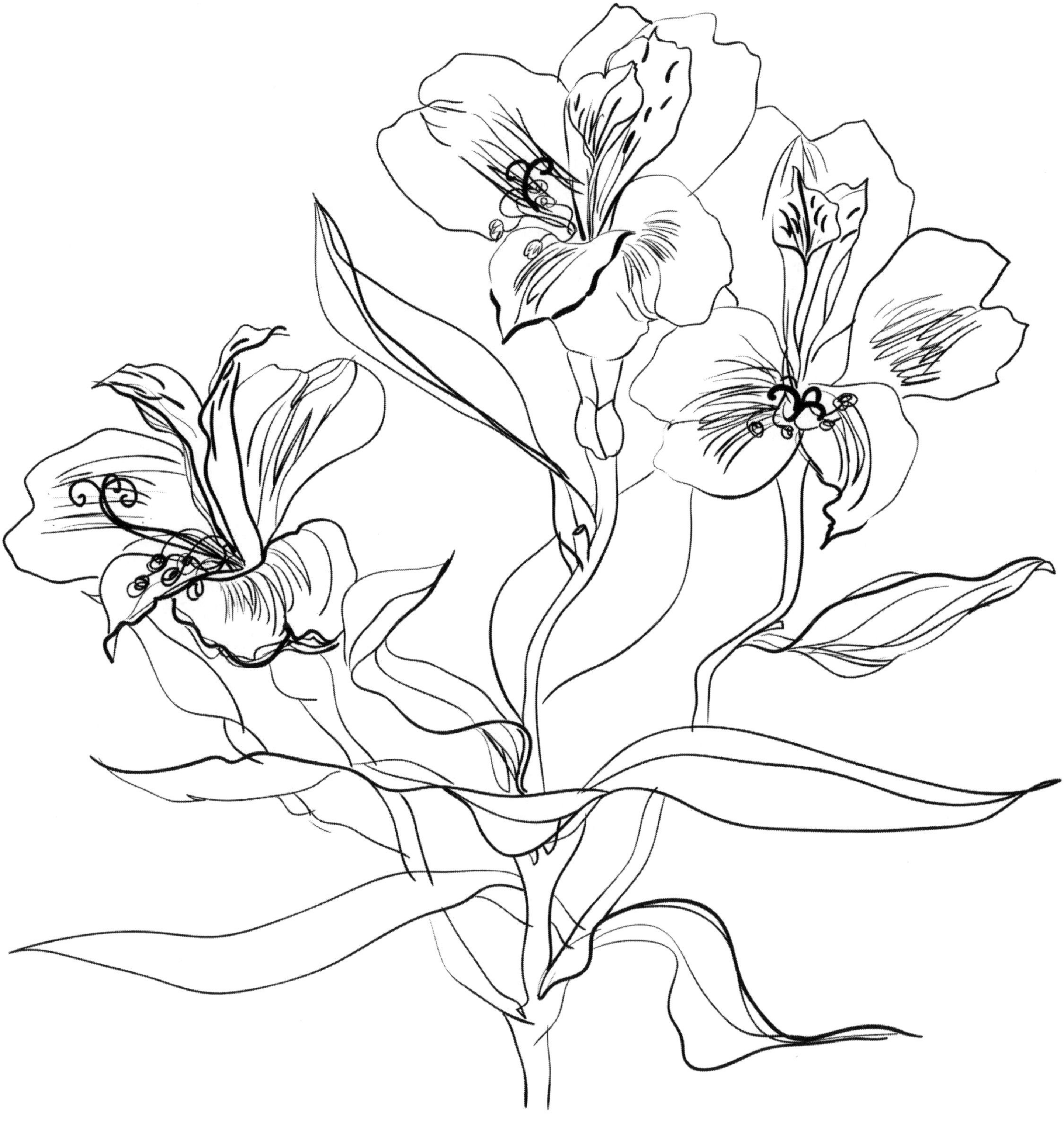

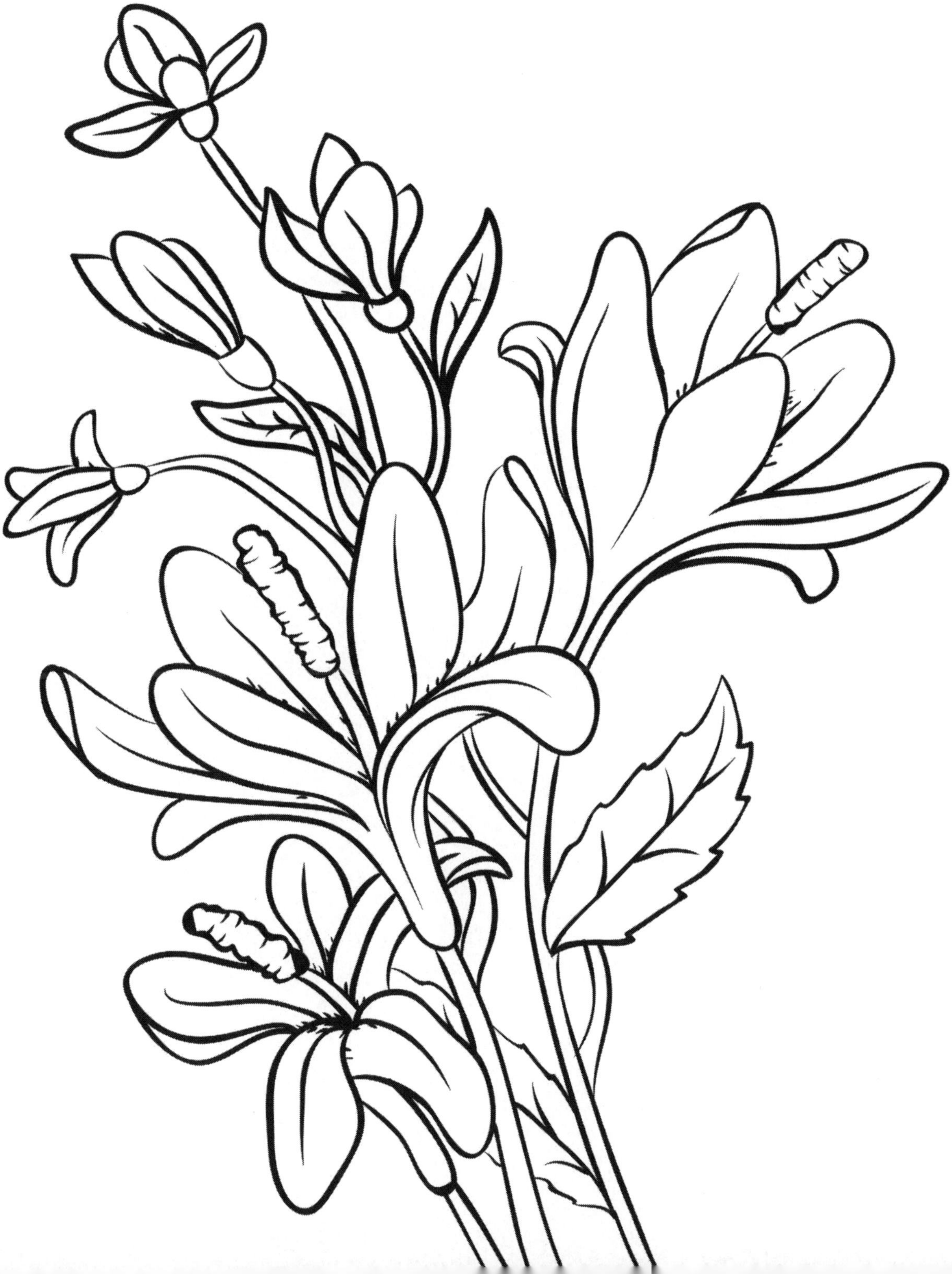

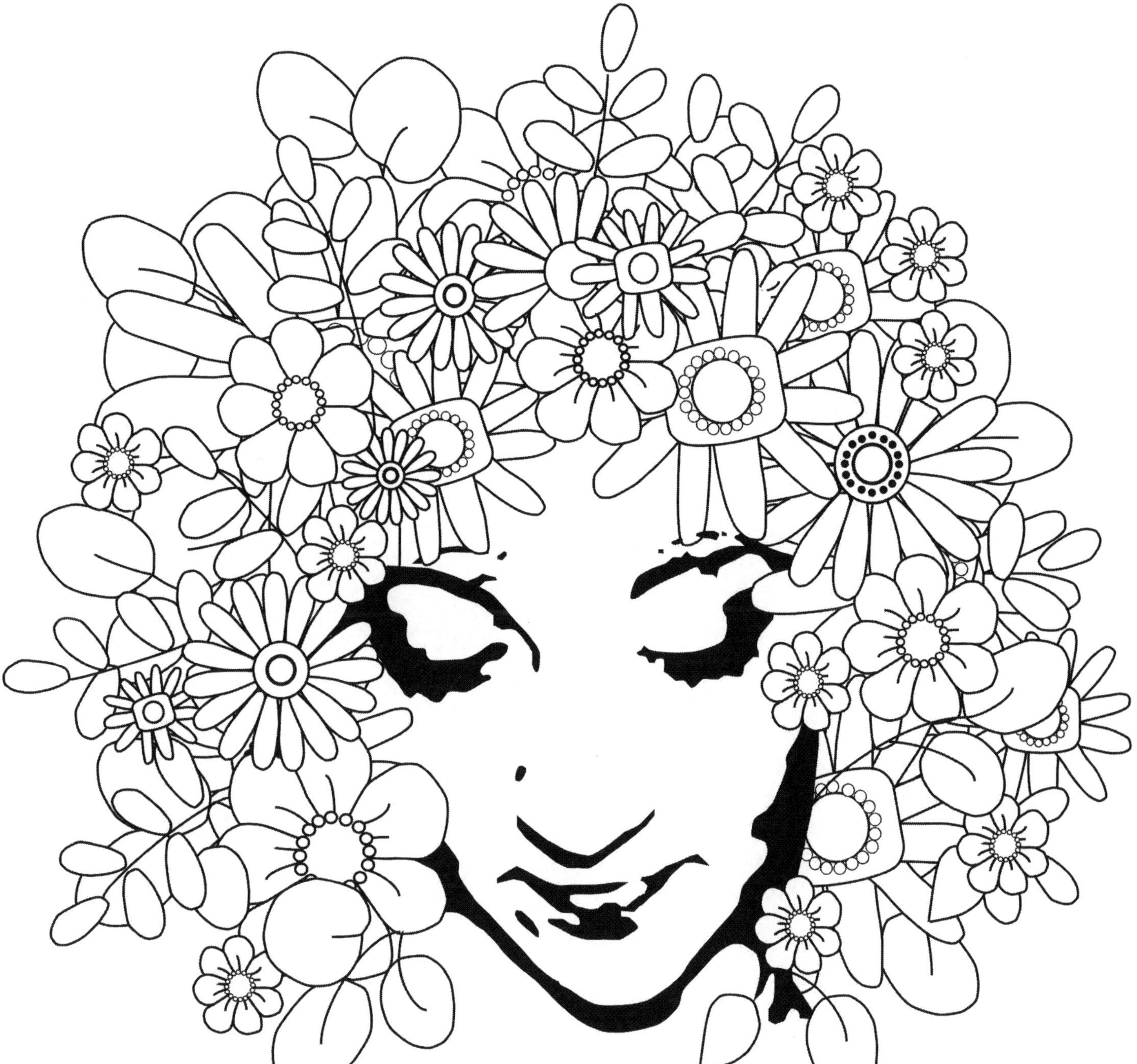